Jenni Dobson

quick and easy Quilts

20 stylish projects for fast results

hamlyn

Dedicated to Len, my husband of thirty-four years, in appreciation of his continuing support and encouragement.

First published in Great Britain in 2006 by
Hamlyn, a division of Octopus Publishing Group Ltd
2–4 Heron Quays, London E14 4JP

Distributed in the United States and Canada by
Sterling Publishing Co., Inc..
387 Park Avenue South, New York, NY 10016–8810

ISBN-13: 978-0-600-61535-4
ISBN-10: 0-600-61535-9

A CIP catalogue record for this book is available from the British Library

Printed and bound in China

10 9 8 7 6 5 4 3 2 1

quick and easy
Quilts

Contents

Introduction

Welcome to a new collection of quick and easy quilts. Twenty stunning projects offer a range of quilts suitable for newcomers to quilt-making and experienced stitchers wanting a speedy project. Sometimes what makes a project quick to do is that it draws on the existing skills of the maker. So, if you are already widely experienced on the sewing machine, projects such as Enchanted Forest (pages 90–93), requiring good machine control, are quicker than if trying the technique for the first time.

HOW TO USE THIS BOOK

It is worth looking through all the quilts in the book before deciding on a particular one and, while doing so, being honest with yourself about your preferences, existing skills and – perhaps most importantly – how much time you can set aside for sewing. For many people, this involves finding a convenient time to set up the sewing machine, perhaps on the dining table, when it may be important to complete all the machine work in one or two sittings. On the other hand, some people choose to do certain tasks by hand, whatever the time limit: you might like to hand-finish quilt bindings while watching evening television, for example, when the time spent will pass unnoticed.

Before starting any work, read through the project to pin-point particular techniques which are unfamiliar to you. With any new technique it is important to invest a little time and a few spare materials in making a practice sample ahead of time. Gather all your supplies, noting that the metric and imperial measurements in the 'you will need' lists are given in the most common units sold. Most quilt-makers also wash cotton fabrics before use, especially those intended for any kind of bed or utility quilt that may need laundering during its working life. In this way you can see whether fabrics are colourfast (see also Caring for quilts, page 131).

It is assumed that you will be using a sewing machine for most of the work, but several of the projects offer a choice to hand-sew some elements (for those who enjoy it and when there is time). For example, a quilt top can be relatively quickly made and then hand-quilted. This is not a speedy task but gives a particular look and feel to the end product. The projects also offer ideas for varying the design shown and, of course, you may well be inspired to make your own variations based on ideas from another project.

MAKING THE MOST OF YOUR SEWING TIME

The secret to making the most of your sewing time lies in being well prepared for a project and in developing efficient working methods.

• Before starting a new project, read through the instructions to make sure you have the necessary materials and equipment. Check that your machine is running properly (with spare needles), and that you have spare blades for your rotary cutter.

• Pre-wash cotton fabrics to check colourfastness and to remove the dressing. Use lukewarm water with a delicate washing product and start with the lightest colours first. Rinse well, dry and iron. Do not pre-wash the various silks or exotics required for some of the projects.

• Make practice samples before starting a project. Making a sample using similar materials allows you to check that you have understood the instructions. You can see which areas need more care in execution and which processes suit a 'production-line' approach.

• Be realistic about how much quilting time you have and what your personal preferences are. If you are not honest with yourself, you are more likely to fail to finish a project. Choosing projects that use techniques you either know or imagine you will enjoy is much more likely to keep your enthusiasm fuelled until completion.

• When making a gift of a quilt for a special occasion do not be tempted to complete the work in a hurry in order to meet a deadline. Instead, give the recipient an envelope with a 'promise' in it and then trade the promise when the quilt has been properly finished.

Classic Quilts

What makes a classic is often wide audience appeal and simplicity of construction, best illustrated by the strip pattern called hit 'n' miss. The basic project uses scraps arranged by value for a modern twist. Other strip-pieced projects include Liberated Log Cabin, Stripy Fish and Chedworth Evergreen, which takes a different angle. Squares are always popular with quilters, and projects here use squares of varied sizes in Country Dance, square-on-point blocks in Cadeaux de Provence and the classic star block in Katharine's Stars. Steamers Ahoy! invites you to experiment with the challenge of accurate piecing using the foundation-pieced method.

Inspired by the region of France famous for its printed textiles, 'Gifts of Provence' is based on the traditional 'square-on-point' block, where the diagonals of the squares dictate the final block size. The simple construction makes the most of the strong colours of the fabrics.

Cadeaux de Provence

APPROXIMATE SIZE OF QUILT

120 x 140 cm (47 x 55 in)

SEAM ALLOWANCES

0.75 cm (¼ in) unless otherwise stated

YOU WILL NEED

A fabric width of 110–114 cm (43–44 in) unless otherwise stated. Iron all fabrics before cutting.

- 30 pre-cut 15 cm (6 in) printed squares
- Six 'fat' quarters (see page 108) minimum of solid colours to complement the printed squares (the quilt shown uses 11 colours in varying quantities)
- 140 cm (54 in) border fabric
- 275 cm (98 in) backing fabric
- 140 cm (54 in) wadding (batting) 150 cm (60 in) wide
- Sewing threads to match
- Invisible thread (optional)
- See also Equipment, pages 110–111

CUTTING

❶ Check the accuracy of the pre-cut squares and trim to make them truly square, if necessary.

❷ Decide which solid colour to set with each printed square, then, from each solid colour (setting) fabric, cut two 15 x 15 cm (6 x 6 in) setting squares per print square. Cut each setting square once diagonally to give four setting triangles. Keep the correct setting triangles with their respective print squares. (If using larger print squares, adjust the size of the setting squares accordingly.)

❸ From the border fabric, cut two 118 x 16.5 cm (46 x 6½ in) strips for the side borders and two 130 x 16.5 cm (51 x 6½ in) strips for the top and bottom borders.

MAKING THE TOP

1 With right sides together, find the centre of the long side of a triangle and match to the centre of one side of a print square. Pin, then, using thread to match either the setting fabric or the print, machine-sew without stretching the bias seam on the triangle. In this way, join two triangles to the opposite sides of a square. Press the seam allowances away from the square before adding the second two triangles to the remaining sides (**Diagram A**). Press. To save time, work in batches, adding the first triangle to all the squares using the same setting colour, then the second triangle, and so on.

2 Make 30 blocks in this way. Spread them out in six rows of five blocks and rearrange them until you are happy with the result. Avoid having two of the same setting fabric next to each other.

3 Follow the instructions for Assembling the quilt top (see pages 120–121) to join the blocks together in horizontal rows. Take care to match the corners of the squares in the blocks when seaming them together (**Diagram B**). Minimize the bulk of the seam allowances by pressing the seams open and trimming projecting points.

4 Now join the rows of blocks, continuing to match the corners of the squares carefully and to press the seams open.

5 Measure the assembled blocks down the centre from top to bottom, to confirm the length needed for the side borders. Mark the quilt-top measurement centrally on to one long edge of each side border strip. On the remaining long edge of each strip, press a 2 cm (¾ in) turning to the wrong side. (This is ready for edge-to-edge finishing.)

6 Follow the instructions for Attaching borders (see page 121) to sew on the first border. Check the fit and press the seam allowances towards the border, then trim the excess length, keeping the outer corners true. Repeat for the opposite border.

7 Now measure the quilt across the centre from left to right, to confirm the length needed for the top and bottom borders. Add 3 cm (1½ in) to this measurement for finishing the quilt edges. Now attach the top and bottom borders in the same way as the side borders. When trimming the excess, remember to leave a 2 cm (¾ in) turning at the ends of these border strips. Press these turnings under so that they align with the border edges running down the sides of the quilt.

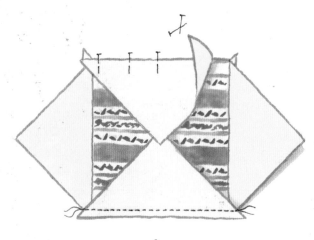

A

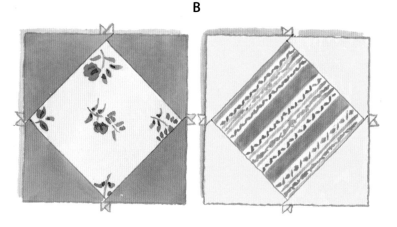

B

ASSEMBLING THE QUILT

1 Follow the instructions for Traditional quilting (see page 122) to prepare the backing fabric and layer the quilt. Assemble the quilt layers and make a small test on scraps of the fabrics used for backing and setting to check your tension and stitch length.

2 Here, the quilt was machine-quilted 'in-the-ditch', where the print squares are seamed to the setting triangles, running diagonally from the square in one block to that in the next. Begin by putting in one diagonal line in each direction and continue to work outwards from these lines in turn. Complete by quilting in the ditch where the borders attach to the centre.

3 Alternatively, this is a good project for hand-quilting if you have the time and inclination. Follow the same quilting plan or one of your own choice. You could also add extra quilting in the borders.

FINISHING

1 The edges of the quilt borders are already pressed for a traditional edge-to-edge finish.

2 Taking care not to damage the fold of the pressed edge, mark, then trim, the wadding to the exact finished size of the quilt. Trim the backing fabric to 2.5 cm (1 in) larger than the wadding.

3 Follow the instructions for Edge-to-edge finishing (see page 129) to complete the quilt.

4 Label the quilt (see page 129) to finish.

Variations

- Choose two setting fabrics, say black and white, and use alternately to give a chequerboard background to your printed squares.
- Packs of printed fabric squares are available in various sizes. Make the quilt using smaller or larger squares, or a different numbers of blocks.

This fresh and clean-looking little quilt would make a cheerful addition to a bright bathroom. Summer always seems to inspire a range of seaside-themed fabrics and you will have plenty of choice available for combining them with a few plaids or stripes to create the desired effect.

Steamers Ahoy!

APPROXIMATE SIZE OF QUILT

60 x 60 cm (24 x 24 in)

SEAM ALLOWANCES

0.75 cm (¼ in) unless otherwise stated

YOU WILL NEED

A fabric width of 110–114 cm (43–44 in) unless otherwise stated. Iron all fabrics before cutting.

- Five 'fat' eighths (see page 108) for foundation-pieced blocks (mottled sky; white funnel; blue/white stripes; solid blue ship; mid-blue sea)
- Three 'fat' eighths seaside-themed fabric for strip-pieced columns
- 70 cm (27 in) seaside-print border fabric
- 70 cm (27 in) backing fabric (includes enough for hanging sleeve)
- 25 cm (10 in) solid yellow for binding and steamer blocks
- 70 cm (27 in) wadding (batting)
- Light blue and yellow sewing threads
- Freezer paper, interfacing or paper for pieced foundation blocks
- 100 cm (40 in) yarn (optional)
- A few small seashells (optional)
- See also Equipment, pages 110–111

CUTTING

① For the foundation-pieced blocks (see below), cut the patches freehand as they are needed for sewing (see page 16).

② From each of the three seaside-themed fat eighths, cut an 11.5 cm (4½ in) strip for piecing the columns. Cut random slices from the strips, none narrower than 4 cm (1½ in).

③ From the border fabric, cut one 63 x 11.5 cm (25 x 4½ in) vertical side border and one 53 x 11.5 cm (21 x 4½ in) vertical side border. For the top and bottom borders, cut two 43 x 11.5 cm (19 x 4½ in) strips across the fabric.

④ From the backing fabric, cut a 65 x 65 cm (26 x 26 in) square.

⑤ From the wadding, cut a 65 x 65 cm (26 x 26 in) square.

⑥ From the binding fabric, cut 5 cm (2 in) strips of yellow to total 250 cm (104 in) when joined

---

TIP
Pictorial fabrics invite cutting selectively to focus on particular areas of the design, for example, taking care to have vertical features placed vertically in the quilt. You may wish to make paper patterns to pin on the fabric in order to check you have made best use of the motifs before cutting.

A

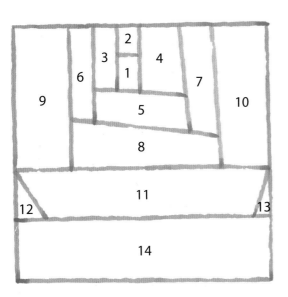

B

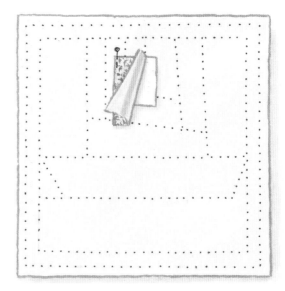

MAKING THE FOUNDATION-PIECED BLOCKS

Foundation-pieced blocks can be worked on a variety of supporting materials. Some, such as calico, remain in the quilt, while others are torn away before the blocks are sewn into the quilt. For the latter, you can use ordinary thin paper, interfacing or – as here – freezer paper. You will be sewing from the back of the work, so please note that the design must be reversed. With freezer paper, the fabric is placed on the waxy side and the stitching worked with the paper side up.

Transfer the block design in **Diagram A** accurately on to six squares of freezer paper. This can be done by tracing with a pencil or by putting one drawn design on top of the six squares and perforating them with your sewing machine without thread in the needle. It is a good idea to staple the layers together (avoiding the drawn lines on the top pattern) so they do not move during machine-perforating.

❶ Load the machine with light blue thread, select a short stitch length and sew the patches in the numbered sequence shown in **Diagram A** using a method known as 'flip-and-sew', as follows. Always cut the fabric pieces sufficiently large to cover the required area plus seam allowances when flipped into place, right side up. If you are new to this technique, make a practice block from scrap materials first.

❷ Cut a small rectangle approximately the size of the funnel (piece 1) plus 0.75 cm (¼ in) all around. Place right side up over the shape on the foundation so that the seam allowances project on all sides. Iron lightly to adhere to the wax. Now cut a rectangle of sky fabric for piece 2 and

place right sides together with piece 1 (**Diagram B**). Pin or hold carefully while turning the unit over and placing under the machine.

❸ Sew exactly on the marked line, extending into the seam allowance at both ends (**Diagram C**). Remove from the machine and flip piece 2 right side up. Check that it extends to meet the top edge of the block – including the seam allowance – before trimming any excess. Press to fix to the waxed surface (**Diagram D**).

❹ Continue in this way, adding pieces 3 and 4 of sky fabric, then piece 5 of striped fabric, and so on. When all the patches have been sewn to the block, press carefully and trim to measure 11.5 cm (4½ in). Repeat the process for the five remaining foundation-pieced blocks.

MAKING THE COLUMNS

❶ Set one foundation-pieced block aside for the quilt border.

❷ Using the seaside-themed cut strips, assemble four columns of patchwork, adding the foundation-pieced blocks, each measuring 41.5 cm (16½ in) from top to bottom. Position the steamers at different levels and note that one column has two steamers. Decide on the order in which the columns will appear in the quilt and number them (see picture on page 15).

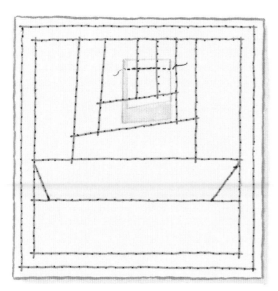

C

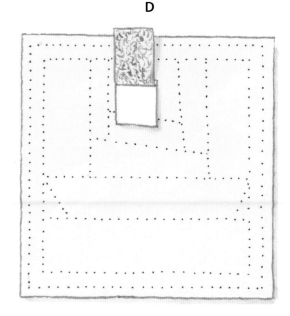

D

ASSEMBLING THE QUILT

1 Follow the instructions for Quilt-as-you-go (see page 125) to layer up and baste together the backing and wadding squares, and then mark the quilt centre both vertically and horizontally with coloured-thread basting.

2 Place column 2, right side up, on the wadding, centred from top to bottom. Have the column edge overlapping the centre line by its seam allowance. Pin along this centre edge.

3 Place column 3, right side down, over column 2, with raw edges level. Pin and sew carefully through all the layers. Flip column 3 right side up and press lightly, covering the wadding with a tea towel. Check that the top and bottom edges are straight and continue to check the edges as you proceed, using a set square and long ruler.

4 Continuing to sew and press the quilt in the same way, attach column 4 and column 1, then the top and bottom borders and the right-hand (long) border.

5 Join the sixth steamer block to the top of the left-hand (short) border. Then, ensuring that the horizontal seam aligns with the top border seam, attach as before.

6 Follow the instructions for Binding (see pages 126–128) to finish the quilt, using the yellow strips already cut.

7 Make and attach a hanging sleeve from the leftover backing fabric, if wished (see page 129), then label the quilt to finish.

OPTIONAL EXTRAS

Sew short lengths of textured yarn by hand to represent smoke from the funnels or attach seashells to the bottom border. Sometimes shells have tiny holes in them, ideal for sewing, otherwise you can make small holes with a needle or fine drill.

Variations

- Use a variety of scraps to make all the steamers look different.
- Replace the seashells with anything from a wide range of nautical buttons and charms.
- Find or design a foundation-pieced block for a yacht to add variety.
- Use a foundation-pieced block of a beach hut to embellish the bottom border.

Hit 'n' miss is an old patchwork pattern. Unlike many pieced designs, where seamed corners or points must meet exactly, none of the seams here needs to match up with any other – hence the name. It is an excellent way to use last scraps of favourite fabrics.

Hit 'n' Miss

APPROXIMATE SIZE OF QUILT
180 x 150 cm (72 x 60 in)

SEAM ALLOWANCES
0.75 cm (¼ in) unless otherwise stated

YOU WILL NEED
A fabric width of 110–114 cm (43–44 in) unless otherwise stated. Iron all fabrics before cutting.
- Scraps approximately equivalent to 325 cm (126 in) for strip-piecing, sorted into light and dark values
- 40 cm (15½ in) dark green cotton for binding
- 375 cm (153 in) backing fabric
- 190 cm (75 in) low-loft wadding (batting) 150 cm (60 in) wide or the size of a single bed
- Neutral sewing thread
- Sewing threads to match backing and binding
- See also Equipment, pages 110–111

CUTTING

❶ From the scraps, where the fabric size permits, cut a number of 16.5 cm (6½ in) wide strips for each value. Not all of each fabric needs to be cut up in this way, because you can cut more strips as you need them while piecing. From some of what is left, cut a number of 9 cm (3½ in) wide strips. Keep the value piles as sorted.

❷ From the binding fabric, cut 5 cm (2 in) strips to total approximately 660 cm (264 in), but do not sew together yet.

❸ From the scraps, choose a few bright solid colours from which to cut short lengths, say 9–14 cm (3½–5½ in) long and 5 cm (2 in) wide, to include in the binding.

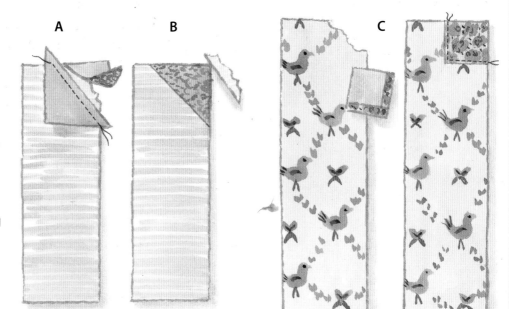

TIP

Extra interest and greater economy can be achieved by adding a patch to the corner·of a piece that is not quite the required size. Two methods for filling a missing corner are shown. In method 1, a square is sewn to the right side of the fabric (**Diagram A**). This is pressed into place and the back trimmed to leave a triangular patch (**Diagram B**). In method 2, a square patch, with seam allowance pressed under as required, is topstitched in place (**Diagram C**).

MAKING THE PIECED STRIPS

1 The basic method is simple: piece together enough 16.5 cm (6½ in) wide strips of the light fabrics to total 183 cm (73 in). Start with two patches of fabric, the required width and any length, placed right sides together and sew down one 16.5 cm (6½ in) side using a neutral thread. Ensure that the outer edges are level and press the seam open. Add patches as desired to either or both ends. If you feel a piece is too long, simply cut it where you like before adding another patch.

2 Make six pieced strips in total – three using the light-coloured strips and three using the dark.

3 Proceed in the same way to make four dark and four light pieced strips using the 9 cm (3½ in) wide patches, each measuring 183 cm (73 in) in length.

4 Press all the finished strips carefully and remove any stray threads (especially dark ones) from the back of them. Spread the strips out so that you can decide on the order in which you prefer to use them.

ASSEMBLING THE QUILT

1 Follow the instructions for Backing fabric (see page 122) to divide the backing fabric in half and join to make up an area 185 x 155 cm (74 x 62 in) for the backing. This is a little oversized to allow for trimming back.

2 Follow the instructions for Quilt-as-you-go (see page 125) to layer up the backing and wadding, and thread-baste across the narrower measurement. Thread-baste a line across one end of the quilt about 2.5 cm (1 in) from the raw edge to represent the expected top edge. Also, use a different colour thread to mark, accurately, a central vertical from which to start attaching the strips.

3 Place the first broad light strip, right side up, down the centre of the quilt-as-you-go layers, having one long raw edge overlapping the basted vertical centre line by 0.75 cm (¼ in) and one end overlapping the basted top line by 1.25 cm (½ in). Pin and thread-baste both long edges of this strip thoroughly. It is essential that this first strip is as straight as you can get it because any wobbles will seem to increase as you proceed.

4 Place a broad dark strip, right sides together, over the light strip with raw edges level and pin closely.

5 With neutral thread in the needle and thread matching the backing fabric in the bobbin, sew through all the layers, taking a 0.75 cm (¼ in) seam allowance. Flip the dark strip right side up and press.

6 Repeat the process, working outwards. Sew a narrow strip on each side of the two central ones, keeping the alternate light and dark sequence correct, then add two wide strips on each side, followed by the two remaining narrow strips to complete the pattern.

7 When all the strips have been added, baste the layers together down the long edges, which should be straight.

8 Starting at the top line (basted in step 2), check that this is still at right angles to the long sides. Trim and baste close to the edge. Repeat to trim the bottom of the quilt.

FINISHING

1 Follow the instructions for Binding (see pages 126–128) to finish the quilt. Note that the binding needs to be sewn 1.25 cm (½ in) from the raw edge and turned in to finish 1.25 cm (½ in) wide. To piece the binding together, join a coloured patch to one end of a dark green strip with a straight seam and press the turnings open. Position the first strip against the quilt edge where you want that bright insert to be and lay the strip around the quilt until you reach where the next should be. Add the second coloured patch, pressing the seam open and trimming the dark green. Proceed in this way to work all around the quilt. Remember to use straight seams for joining the ends of bright colours, but a diagonal seam for joining the dark green strips together.

2 Label the quilt (see page 129) to finish.

> **TIP**
> Another method of using assorted small scraps is to sew together a few of them in any manner to make a 16.5 cm (6½ in) wide unit of any length. This can be tidied into a neat rectangle before being included in the main strip.

Variations

- Piece the 'light' strips from white-on-white, white-on-cream or off-white fabrics, then use a mix of brights and darks for the 'dark' strips.
- Choose a single dark fabric, patterned or solid, from which to cut all the 'dark' strips then use a mix of pieced scraps in lights and brights for the 'light' strips.

This pattern uses the 'eight-pointed star' block set into background strips and can be made quickly from a collection of brightly coloured scraps and with just two lengths of fabric for the strips. Quick piecing methods are used to make the blocks, and some have a pieced centre detail for added interest.

Katharine's Stars

APPROXIMATE SIZE OF QUILT

147.5 x 140 cm (58 x 56 in)

SEAM ALLOWANCES

0.75 cm (¼ in) unless otherwise stated

YOU WILL NEED

A fabric width of 110–114 cm (43–44 in) unless otherwise stated. Iron all fabrics before cutting.

- Scrap fabric approximately equivalent to 150 cm (60 in) of bright and dark prints for the star blocks and the small strips of squares. The largest scrap need only be 15 cm (6 in) square
- Two 100 cm (39 in) light- or medium-toned prints for background strips (beige and light blue-violet were used here)
- 173 x 162.5 cm (68 x 64 in) backing fabric (here pieced from oddments)
- 50 cm (19½ in) pale-blue marbled print for binding
- 173 x 162.5 cm (68 x 64 in) low-loft wadding (batting)
- Neutral sewing thread
- Variegated machine-embroidery or quilting thread (optional)
- See also Equipment, pages 110–111

CUTTING

1 For each different star block, work as follows. From the scrap fabric, choose one fabric for the stars and one for the sky. From the star fabric, cut one 11.5 cm (4½ in) square for centre square A (**Diagram C** overleaf) and four 7.25 (2⅞) squares. From the sky fabric, cut four 6.25 cm (2½ in) squares for corner squares B and one 13.5 cm (5¼ in) square. A total of 11 star blocks is needed for the quilt, of which three in our example have pieced centres (see below).

2 For a pieced centre, first decide whether the centre square-on-point will be sky or star fabric and cut one A square to the size above. Cut four B squares from the contrast fabric.

3 For the pieced strips, cut forty 6.25 cm (2½ in) squares from bright colour scraps.

4 From the two 100 cm (39 in) pieces of light or medium fabric, cut across from selvedge to selvedge to make four 21.5 cm (8½ in) background strips. These should be the same width as the pieced blocks, so you may wish to make the blocks and check their size before cutting them.

5 From the pale-blue marbled print, cut 6.25 cm (2½ in) wide strips for binding to a total of 600 cm (240 in) when joined

MAKING A STAR BLOCK

1 Start by making the 'flying geese' units for the block: mark both diagonals on a large sky square, right side up, and mark one diagonal on the wrong side of each of the four little star squares.

2 Place two little star squares, right side down, on opposite corners of the right side of the sky square, aligning the diagonals. Sew both sides of the diagonal, taking a standard seam allowance (**Diagram A**). Cut apart along the diagonal and press the little patches right side up.

3 Place another little star square in the remaining corner of each patch. Again, sew both sides of the diagonal, cut along it to separate, and press (**Diagram B**). You now have four flying geese, or C pieces.

4 Lay out the A and B squares and the C pieces on a flat surface and stitch together in the sequence illustrated by the arrows in **Diagram C**.

5 For a pieced centre, cut four 6.5 cm (2½ in) squares. Mark a diagonal on the wrong side of each. With square A right side up, place a little square right side down on a corner with the diagonal running across the corner not into it. Sew along the diagonal. Press the triangle right side up and trim the excess below to the usual seam allowance. Repeat on the remaining corners. Make the C pieces as above.

6 Make a total of 11 blocks, some with a pieced centre. Each block should measure 21.5 x 21.5 cm (8½ x 8½ in).

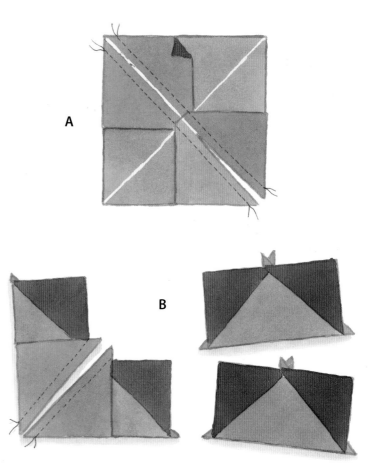

A

B

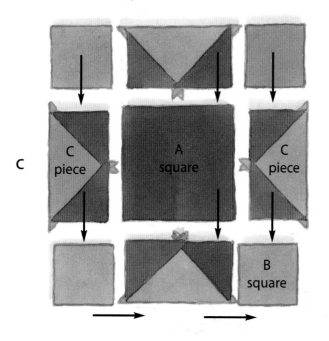

C

C piece   A square   C piece

B square

ASSEMBLING THE QUILT TOP

1 For the pieced strips of small squares, stitch together four 6.25 cm (2½ in) squares in a line. Press. Ten sets are needed. (If the star blocks come out oversize, these strips will need extending by an extra patch).

2 Assemble the quilt in strips, working from left to right and referring to the quilt plan in **Diagram D** as a guide for cutting the lengths of background strips and for inserting the star blocks and pieced strips of squares. The measurements (which include 0.75 cm/¼ in for seam allowances).are a guide and can be changed.

3 Continue to assemble the strips and blocks, noting that every other strip has one star block and two strips of squares besides being of an alternate background colour. Press seams away from the blocks or strips. When all the strips are stitched, you may have to straighten the top and bottom edges.

4 Sew the strips together to complete the quilt top, then press.

QUILTING AND FINISHING

1 For a quilt of this size, a long-arm quilting service is a good option. Alternatively, follow the instructions for Traditional quilting (see pages 122–123) to layer up the top, wadding and backing, and baste.

2 Using the Free-machine quilting method (see page 119) and referring to the picture as a guide, quilt over the surface of the quilt in variegated machine-quilting thread.

3 Trim the backing and wadding level with the edges of the quilt and follow the directions for Double binding (see pages 126–128) to finish the quilt.

4 Label the quilt (see page 129) to finish.

Variations

- Assemble the quilt top using the Quilt-as-you-go method (see page 125). As these strips are quite wide, add a little extra quilting, perhaps horizontally along the block-and-background strip seams.

- Substitute a different block design or use 'orphan' blocks left from other projects. If blocks finish a different size, change the width of the background strips to match. If so, adjust the pieced strips of little squares too.

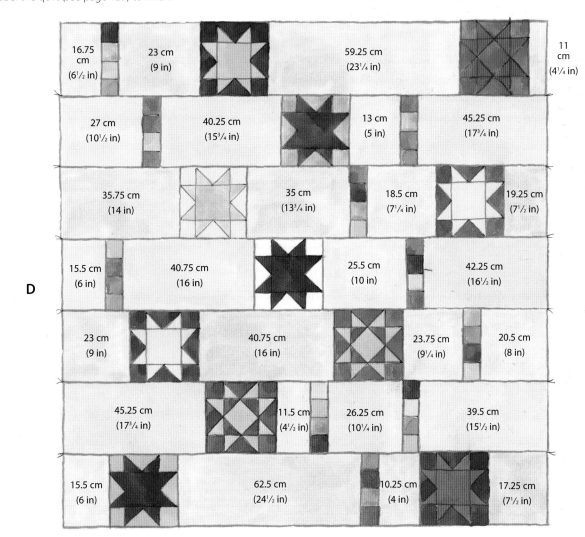

This is a great way of using up scraps remaining from other projects. It also makes a suitable group project, where each person sews a couple of strips, then exchanges them with another stitcher, ensuring that everyone's strips are spread throughout the quilt.

Liberated Log Cabin

APPROXIMATE SIZE OF QUILT

120 x 150 cm (48 x 60 in)

SEAM ALLOWANCES

0.75 cm (¼ in) unless otherwise stated

YOU WILL NEED

A fabric width of 110–114 cm (43–44 in) unless otherwise stated. Iron all fabrics before cutting.

- 250 cm (100 in) backing fabric (or equivalent in pieces)
- 100 cm (39 in) red cotton fabric for binding, sashing and patches
- 19 assorted 'fat' quarters (see page 108) or equivalent in strips from a comprehensive scrap bag
- 200 cm (81 in) wadding (batting) 150 cm (60 in) wide
- Red sewing thread to match red fabric
- Sewing thread to match backing fabric
- See also Equipment, pages 110–111

CUTTING

❶ From the backing fabric, cut twelve 31.5 x 31.5 cm (12½ x 12½ in) squares. For the border blocks, cut fourteen 31.5 x 16.5 cm (12½ x 6½ in) rectangles and four 16.5 x 16.5 cm (6½ x 6½ in) squares.

❷ Also from the backing fabric, cut the following for sashing: eight 31.5 x 3.25 cm (12½ x 1¼ in) strips, three 91.5 x 3.25 cm (36½ x 1¼ in) strips, fourteen 16.5 x 3.25 cm (6½ x 1¼ in) strips and four 121.5 x 3.25 cm (48½ x 1¼ in) strips.

❸ From the red fabric, cut 3.25 cm (1¼ in) wide strips to total 570 cm (228 in) of binding when joined.

❹ Also from the red fabric, cut a set of sashing strips for the front of the quilt exactly as listed above for the backing fabric sashing strips.

❺ Still from the red fabric, cut six 10 x 10 cm (4 x 4 in) squares and cut in half once diagonally for the centre triangles of the square blocks. Cut eighteen 6.25 cm (2½ in) squares for the centre squares of the border blocks.

❻ Cut the fat quarters into a variety of strips from 2.5 cm (1 in) to 6.5 cm (2½ in) wide, approximately. The strips need not have parallel sides – they can be wedge-shaped.

❼ From the wadding, cut twelve 34.5 x 34.5 cm (13½ x 13½ in) squares, fourteen 34.5 x 19.5 cm (13½ x 7½ in) rectangles and four 19.5 x 19.5 cm (7½ x 7½ in) squares.

MAKING THE BLOCKS

1 Baste together each large backing square, right side down, with a slightly larger square of wadding on top. These squares will form the centre of the quilt. Six rows of basting spaced across these large blocks in one direction is enough to hold them together.

2 Similarly, layer together and baste the rectangles of backing and wadding for the borders and the little squares of backing and wadding for the border corners.

3 Starting with one large square block, place a red triangle, right side up and roughly in the centre, on the wadding. Place a fabric strip, right side down, on any side of the triangle, with raw edges level (**Diagram A**). Pin and stitch through all the layers. If wished, reverse-sew at the seam ends unless the seam reaches the edge of the wadding. Flip the strip right side up and press with your finger.

4 Sew a strip of a different fabric to another side of the triangle in the same way (**Diagram B**). It does not matter in which order the sides are sewn.

5 Continue to add strips randomly – any width, any order, any direction, any shape – until the whole area is covered. If a strip is not quite long enough to accommodate the diagonal side, simply sew another strip across to cover the ends. This can add another 'side' on which to build. Sometimes an odd triangle from a scrap bag will be useful for a corner.

6 If necessary, to hold the final patches right side up correctly at the edge or corner, add a bar-tack by hand or machine in the expected seam allowance.

7 Turn the block over and remove the basting from the backing. Lay the block right side down on a cutting mat and trim it to 30 cm (12 in) square, making sure that the fabric in the corners is lying flat.

8 Make another 11 blocks in the same way, but change the orientation of the red triangle each time and use as many different fabrics as possible.

9 Make the border blocks, both rectangles and squares, in the same way but starting with a red square instead of a triangle.

10 Trim the 14 completed rectangles to 30 x 15 cm (12 x 6 in) and the four corner squares to 15 x 15 cm (6 x 6 in).

A

B

C

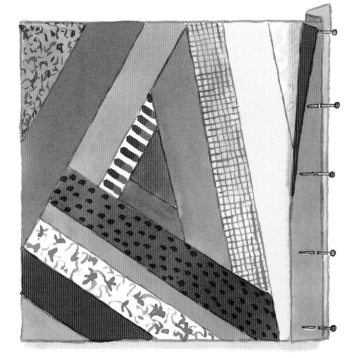

D

ASSEMBLING THE QUILT

❶ Spread out all of the blocks and decide on a pleasing arrangement. You will first assemble the central 12 square blocks as four rows of three.

❷ Begin with the top-left block, working on the right-hand edge that will be joined to the second block in row 1. Pin a 31.5 cm (12½ in) red sashing strip, right side down, on the front of the block and a back sashing strip, right side down, on the back of the block. Sew through all the layers (**Diagram C**).

❸ Now place only the back sashing strip, right side down, on the back of the second block and sew (**Diagram D**). When the blocks are laid flat, the trimmed block edges should butt together smoothly.

❹ Finger-press the red sashing over the raw edges of the seams and turn under a hem, using the stitching line from the back sashing as a guide (**Diagram E**). Pin or baste.

❺ Top-stitch this hem in place using matching red thread, then top-stitch the opposite side of the red sashing strip for a more balanced finish. Take time to do this carefully then trim the excess sashing.

❻ Add a third block in the same way, then make three more rows of blocks. Using the 91.5 cm (36½ in) sashing strips, join the rows of blocks together using the same method.

❼ Repeat the process to assemble the two side borders, each of four rectangles joined with 16.5 cm (6½ in) sashing strips, and join to the sides of the quilt centre, using 121.5 cm (48½ in) sashing.

❽ Make the top and bottom borders from three rectangular blocks with a small corner square at each end and attach in the same way.

E

FINISHING

1 Follow the instructions for Binding (pages 126–128) to finish the quilt, but note that you need to sew the binding to the back of the quilt first, taking a 0.75 cm (¼ in) turning. Bring it over to the front and turn in the raw edge and pin or baste as preferred. Then top-stitch in red thread to match the sashing.

2 Label the quilt (see page 129) to finish.

Variations

- The quilt dimensions are easy to change, either by altering the block size or just by adding another row or more of blocks. Remember to add the necessary rectangular border blocks if choosing the latter.

- Vary the sashing colour, or start with different shapes in the centres of the blocks.

- Create an economical and interesting version by using squares of different fabrics for the block backings instead of buying by the metre (yard). Choosing a single solid-colour fabric for the back sashing would still pull them together effectively.

This is one of the simplest projects in the book and features stylized fish cut from fabric that has been strip-pieced. The fish and seaweed are fused in place and the whole background simply quilted. You can easily resize this project to suit a particular space or a special length of 'watery' fabric.

Stripy Fish

APPROXIMATE SIZE OF QUILT
111 x 145 cm (43½ x 57 in)

SEAM ALLOWANCES
0.75 cm (¼ in) unless otherwise stated

YOU WILL NEED
A fabric width of 110–114 cm (43–44 in) unless otherwise stated. Iron all fabrics before cutting.
- Six 'fat' quarters (see page 108) of assorted batik or space-dyed fabrics in a rainbow of colours for strip-piecing and seaweed
- 150 cm (60 in) background 'sea' fabric, suitable for use sideways
- 175 cm (69 in) backing fabric
- 150 cm (60 in) sewable fusible webbing
- 150 cm (60 in) low-loft wadding (batting)
- 800 cm (320 in) approximately narrow ribbon
- Sewing thread and machine-embroidery thread
- Baking parchment (optional)
- Templates on page 134
- See also Equipment, pages 110–111

CUTTING

❶ From the rainbow-coloured scraps, cut strips of varying width, including some that taper.

❷ Also from the rainbow-coloured scraps, cut straight 3 cm (1⅛ in) wide strips, in a mix of colours, to total 535 cm (212 in) when joined for binding.

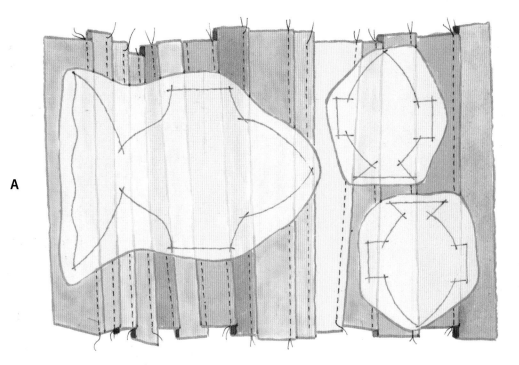

A

MAKING THE FISH

1 Make one card template for each of the fish and jellyfish patterns on page 134. Read the instructions for Appliqué (see pages 116–117).

2 Draw around a number of fish and jellyfish and some strands of seaweed on to the paper side of the fusible webbing, remembering that the motifs need to be reversed. This project has five small fish, three large ones and two jellyfish, but you can vary this number. Cut out each shape with a small margin all around.

3 Sew together fabric strips to build up a large enough area for cutting out several fish. Press all the seams in one direction.

4 Working on the ironing board, place the strip-pieced fabric right side down and arrange some fish shapes upon it, paper side up (**Diagram A**). Cover the shapes with baking parchment, if using, and follow the manufacturer's directions for using the product to fuse the fish shapes to the strip-pieced fabric.

5 When cool, cut out the fish along the drawn outlines (**Diagram B**).

6 Repeat steps 3 to 5 to make as many fish and jellyfish as you require, as well as a few strands of seaweed.

B

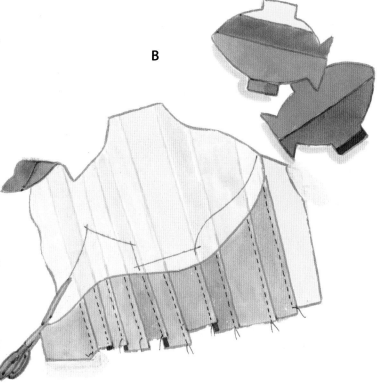

APPLIQUÉING THE FISH

1 Iron the background fabric and decide which way up it will be used. Arrange the fish on it with the seaweed growing up from the bottom edge. Having decided where the jellyfish are to be, cut lengths of ribbon and tuck them under the bottom edge of each jellyfish shape, and pin. The ribbons are of different lengths but each jellyfish has eight pieces.

2 When you are satisfied with the arrangement, peel the backing from a few of the shapes at a time and fuse them into place until they are all attached. Gently gather the ribbons together on each jellyfish and secure them out of the way for the following steps.

3 Follow the instructions for Machine-embroidery (see pages 118–119) to set up your machine and work zigzag or satin stitch around each shape. Three different colours were used on this project but a single, variegated thread would be equally successful. Sewing the seaweed with a thread to match the background fabric gives the illusion that it is waving in the water.

ASSEMBLING AND QUILTING

1 Mark wavy lines in a loosely interlocking pattern on the quilt top, crossing the fish as necessary, using the template on page 132. The design does not have to repeat exactly.

2 Follow the instructions for Assembling the quilt top (see pages 120– 121). There should be a strip of backing fabric left over for making a sleeve.

3 Follow the instructions for Machine-quilting (see page 123) and use your drawn lines as a guide to machine-quilt the wavy lines, continuing over the fish but avoiding catching the jellyfish ribbons.

FINISHING

1 Trim the edges of the quilt to be straight and the corners square, if necessary.

2 Follow the instructions on Binding (see pages 126–128) to finish the quilt, using the rainbow binding strips, to a 0.75 cm (¼ in) finish.

3 Release the jellyfish ribbons and, making a few small stitches at intervals by hand, attach some of the ribbons in coils and loops. Leave some unattached.

4 Make and attach a hanging sleeve from leftover fabric, if wished (see page 129). Note that, since the height of the quilt is also the width of the fabric used, the strip of backing left over will be shorter than the width of the quilt. This means dividing the fabric into two equal halves to make up as two sleeves, each of which can be sewn towards one end of the quilt. Ensure that they are level.

5 Label the quilt (see page 129) to finish.

Variations

- Look out for sea prints for the background, especially those that shade from light to dark. Alternatively, it might be possible to find prints that resemble seaweed or coral formations.

- Strip-piece the fabric in such a way that all of the fish are identical.

- Encourage children to get involved by asking them to draw the fish shapes.

This little machine-made quilt uses six fat quarters of fabric purchased as a coordinating bundle. In the original colour scheme there were two greens, two reds, a beige and a red/beige, but beginners may find it easier to start with two values of each of three colours.

Country Dance

APPROXIMATE SIZE OF QUILT

90 x 90 cm (36 x 36 in)

SEAM ALLOWANCES

0.75 cm (¼ in) unless otherwise stated

YOU WILL NEED

A fabric width of 110–114 cm (43–44 in) unless otherwise stated. Iron all fabrics before cutting.

- 6 'fat' quarters (see page 108) of fabric for the patchwork, measuring at least 50 x 55 cm (19½ in x 22 in): two values in each of three colours: dark and light red, dark and light green and dark and light beige
- 100 cm (39 in) backing fabric
- 50 cm (19½ in) sewable fusible webbing
- 100 cm (39 in) low-loft cotton wadding (batting)
- Neutral sewing thread
- Decorative machine threads for the appliqué (optional)
- See also Equipment, pages 110–111

CUTTING

1 From each of the fat quarters, cut sixteen 11.5 cm (4½ in) squares to make a total of 96 (**Diagram A** overleaf). You may be able to stack your fabrics to cut the squares but you must cut accurately in order to have enough fabric left for the little squares and the binding. Take care not to cut into the remaining fabric, and put this to one side.

2 Cut the backing fabric into a 100 cm (39 in) square.

3 Cut the wadding into a 100 cm (39 in) square.

A

MAKING THE QUILT BACKGROUND

❶ Arrange the squares into nine nine-patch blocks, as shown in the background of **Diagram B**, or by alternating dark and light values in any way you prefer. This leaves 15 squares remaining, which you will use for the binding.

❷ Follow the instructions on Patchwork techniques (see pages 114–115) to chain-piece the squares in rows, and stitch the rows together, pressing the seams open throughout.

PREPARING THE BINDING

It is best to do this before cutting the little squares, since all of the remaining fabric will then be available for the appliqué.

❶ Arrange the 15 remaining squares randomly in three rows of five. Place a different fabric at each row end, because the rows will be joined to one another later.

❷ Stitch the squares in each row together as laid out and press the seams open.

❸ Using a rotary cutter and ruler, cut each row of five squares lengthwise into three 3.75 cm (1½ in) wide strips (see Rotary cutting techniques, pages 112–113). You will now have nine strips.

❹ Join eight strips into four pairs at random, one pair for each side of the quilt. This makes four strips of binding each containing ten squares.

MAKING THE APPLIQUÉ

All the remaining fabric can now be used for the little squares. You should still have enough of the original fabrics to contain a 45 x 7.5 cm (18 x 3 in) unit. This depends on the width of the selvedge. **Do not cut out your squares yet.** If you can fit in this size rectangle on each fabric, you will have lots of choice as to which colours and design you wish to use. Even if you can manage to fit in only two columns of squares side by side you will have enough squares to follow the design shown in **Diagram B**. You will also be able to cut a few more squares from the unwanted strip of binding to give a bit more flexibility in colour placement.

❶ Follow the instructions for Appliqué techniques (see pages 116–117). On the paper side of the fusible webbing, draw six 45 x 7.5 cm (18 x 3 in) rectangles slightly separated from each other (or 45 x 5 cm/18 x 2 in if this is all your fabric permits). Cut out each rectangle with a small margin all around. Iron on to the wrong side of the six fabric pieces according to the manufacturer's instructions.

❷ With the paper side up, cut out each rectangle accurately using a rotary cutter. Turn fabric side up then cut each rectangle lengthwise into three 2.5 cm (1 in) wide strips. Remove the backing paper and cut the strips into 2.5 cm (1 in) squares, as required, with the sticky side of the fabric up.

❸ Arrange the little squares on each pieced block. Note that in each case two of the units are counterchanged with the squares behind them – so red sits on green and green on red, etc.

❹ It is a good idea to lay out all the little squares before bonding them, in order to establish a pleasing distribution of colours. If you wish to use different arrangements of squares, try to place them in groups to minimize the amount of quilting needed.

❺ When you are satisfied with the design, bond the little squares to the pieced blocks according to the manufacturer's instructions, making sure that they butt up against one another closely at the seams and are at 90 degress to one another. A transparent ruler helps here.

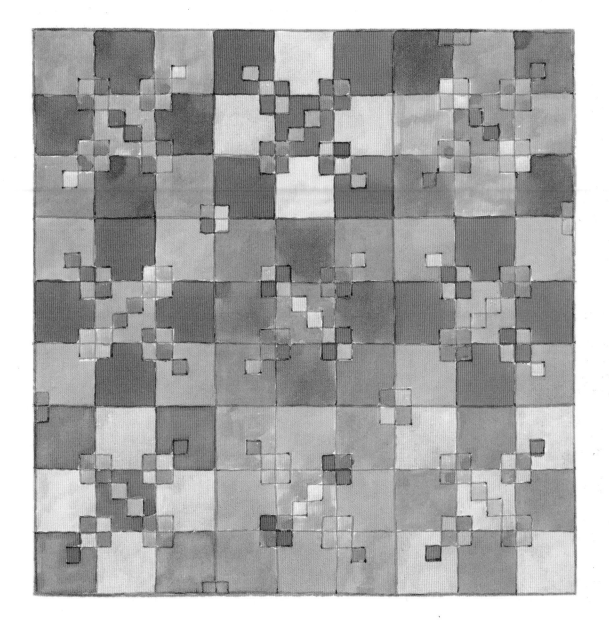

6 Follow the instructions for Machine-embroidery (see pages 118–119) and use a fine, open zigzag stitch (2.5 width and 1.0 length, for example) and a regular or embroidery foot on the machine, to stitch along the lines where the squares abut, making sure that the stitching catches in the pieces of fabric on both sides. Stitch only these junctions: do not stitch around the outside of the squares yet, as this will be part of the quilting. Stop and start with a couple of stitches on the spot or use the tying-off facility if available on your machine. Pull threads through and snip off. These ends will be stitched over again later. Press again.

ASSEMBLING AND QUILTING

1 Follow the instructions for Assembling the quilt top (see pages 120–121) to layer up the backing, wadding and top. Avoid pinning the edges of the bonded squares because you will stitch around those first.

2 Follow the instructions for Machine-quilting (see page 123). Using the same size of zigzag as before and a walking foot if you have one, stitch around the groups of squares in a route that minimizes stops and starts. Start in the centre of the quilt and, having secured all the squares, echo-quilt once or twice more around the groups using just the width of your sewing-machine foot as a guide and continuing to stitch with the same size of zigzag. If using plaids, and the lines are at right angles to one another, you can use them as guidelines. Add more quilting as desired, then press.

BINDING AND FINISHING

1 Follow the instructions for Binding (see pages 126–128) to prepare the quilt edges, as directed on page 126, then trim away the excess backing and wadding. Note that this project is bound in a specific way to suit the design.

2 Take one of the four strips of binding and pin, right sides together and with raw edges level, along one edge of the back of the quilt, offsetting the seam lines so that each falls at the centre of a square along the edge of the quilt.

3 Machine with a 0.75 cm (¹/₄ in) seam, starting and stopping 0.75 cm (¹/₄ in) from each end.

4 With the back of the quilt still facing upwards, fold the binding in half so that the raw edge meets the seam line, and press.

5 Fold the binding over so that the crease meets the seam line on the front and the raw edge is tucked under the seam (**Diagram C**). Pin or baste in place.

6 Repeat on the other three sides and trim as desired to make square or mitred corners, then stitch the corners in place.

7 Stitch along the edge of the binding on the front of the quilt with the same zigzag as used previously, covering the seam line on the back at the same time.

8 Make and attach a hanging sleeve from leftover fabric and label the quilt (see page 129) to finish.

C

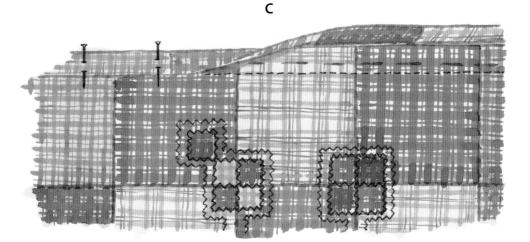

This version of the hit 'n' miss pattern (see also pages 18–21) was inspired by the wall of a Roman villa. This wall used pieces of stone of varying size, organized into courses that alternated between straight and sloping. For the best effect, avoid having the same fabric in two neighbouring patches.

Chedworth Evergreen

APPROXIMATE SIZE OF QUILT

137 x 112 cm (54 x 44 in)

SEAM ALLOWANCES

0.75 cm (¼ in) unless otherwise stated

YOU WILL NEED

A fabric width of 110–114 cm (43–44 in) unless otherwise stated. Iron all fabrics before cutting.

- Three 45 cm (18 in) flannel prints for strip-piecing
- 13 'fat' quarters (see page 108) of flannel prints for strip-piecing
- 190 cm (72 in) backing fabric
- 120 cm (45 in) dark green flannel print for binding and sashing
- Three 115 x 50 cm (45 x 20 in) rectangles of wadding (batting)
- Neutral sewing thread (or to match backing)
- See also Equipment, pages 110–111

CUTTING

1 From the flannel prints (including the dark green), cut a few strips from the long edges of each for the strip-piecing. Vary the strip widths between 4 cm (1½ in) and 7 cm (2¾ in). Strips cut from full-width fabric can be cut in half. For this example, two wide and two narrow strips were cut from each fabric to start. Cut more as needed.

2 From the backing fabric, cut three 50 cm (19½ in) pieces across the full width of the fabric. Also cut two 5.5 cm (2 in) wide strips, also across the width, for neatening the panel joins on the back of the quilt.

3 From the dark green flannel, cut six 11.5 cm (4 in) wide strips across the full width of the fabric for binding; also cut four 5.5 cm (2 in) wide strips for sashing. (Note: If the fabric is narrower than the backing you have chosen, a fifth strip may be needed to make up the four to the required length.)

MAKING THE PATCHWORK

① To make the A units, sew strips together into random-pieced sets, having two sets in progress at the same time for best efficiency. Off-set the end of the second strip down from the first by the width of a strip (**Diagram A**), to make a set that slopes from top left to bottom right. Make two sets sloping the same way approximately 60 cm (24 in) wide when measured as shown in **Diagram A**. Press the seams in one direction.

② Place a set on the cutting mat and trim the stepped edge, having placed the ruler's 45-degree line on the edge of the bottom strip. From the trimmed edge, measure and cut a pieced strip that is 16.5 cm (6½ in) wide. Provided the original fabric was wide enough, you should be able to cut another set of the same width. If not, cut a 9 cm (3½ in) wide set for the narrow B unit. Treat the second pieced set in exactly the same way.

③ One strip from each set can now be sewn together, stepping down by the width of a strip at the seam, to make a complete A unit. Check that each A unit, when measured between the two shortest points, will extend the full width of the quilt backing. If short, add more stepped-down strips at either or both ends. One completed A unit will be used for the middle panel and the other for an end panel (**Diagram B**).

④ Repeat the process to work two more A units, but stepping the strips up by the width of a strip instead of down, so that they slope in the opposite direction.

⑤ Using the same method, make two narrow B units sloping each way.

⑥ Now make the brick-row C units. Cut 15.5 x 7.5 cm (6 x 2½ in) bricks from the remaining fabrics: seven are needed for the centre row; the other rows need six whole bricks plus two half bricks per row. Cut 4 cm (1½ in) 'mortar' strips. Sew one short end of each brick to a mortar strip, one after another (**Diagram C**), pressing the seams

B

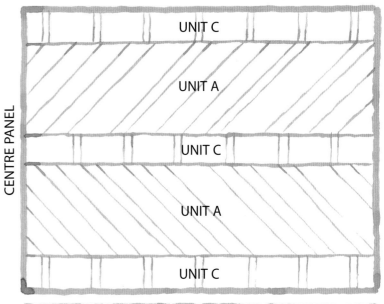

END PANEL

UNIT B

DARK GREEN SASHING STRIP

UNIT B

UNIT A

DARK GREEN SASHING STRIP

CENTRE PANEL

UNIT C

UNIT A

UNIT C

UNIT A

UNIT C

AS OTHER END PANEL BUT REVERSED

A

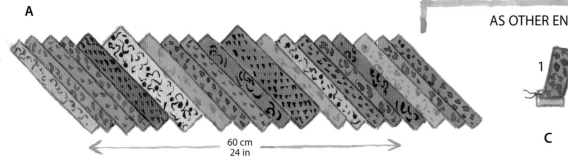

60 cm
24 in

1

C

2 3 4 5 6 7

towards the bricks. Cut apart straight between the bricks, then sew them together to form a course of bricks. Check for length again. The centre row has a brick in the middle while the outer rows have a central mortar strip.

7 The remaining strip-pieced rows are randomly worked using what fabric remains. Two rows need to be cut 7.25 cm (2¾ in) wide and two 5.5 cm (2 in) wide. Ensure the best distribution of fabric by comparing with their neighbouring units as you work.

ASSEMBLING THE QUILT

1 Follow the instructions for Quilt-as-you-go (see page 125) to layer up the backing rectangles and wadding accordingly. Thread-baste the layers parallel to the selvedges.

2 Following **Diagram B**, arrange the pieced rows to check that everything has been made. Include the dark green sashing strips, joined, if necessary, to achieve the required length.

3 Follow the entire-quilt method to attach the units and strips to the backing panels, starting with the middle panel. Position the centre C unit, ensuring that it is straight, and baste both long edges. Then attach the A units to each side, followed by the remaining C units.

4 The end panels are mirror images of each other. Starting at the bottom edge of the top panel, position a green sashing strip, as straight as possible, close to the edge and baste. Now add a pieced A unit and work your way up the panel. Repeat the process for the bottom panel, starting with the dark green sashing at the top edge.

5 Trim the short ends of the three panels, if necessary, so that they are all the same length. Trim the long edges level with the piecing. Thread-baste each outer edge so that all the layers behave as one.

6 Place two sections right sides together, ends and raw edges level, pin frequently and sew. Repeat to attach the third panel. Press the seams open lightly and trim the wadding between layers.

FINISHING

1 Follow the directions for finishing Coffee and Cream (see page 81) to prepare the backing strips, and then use them to neaten the back of the seams.

2 Using the 11.5 cm (4 in) wide dark green strips, follow the instructions for Binding (see pages 126–128) to finish the quilt. Note that this binding is to finish 2.5 cm (1 in) wide. The strips are wide enough to be sewn on 2.5 cm (1 in) from the raw edge, which also means stopping this far from the approaching edge at the corners. A longer gap must be left for joining the tails at the end.

3 Label the quilt (see page 129) to finish.

Variations

- The panels in this project feature three basic pieced-strip designs, any of which can be worked to different measurements or omitted if they do not appeal. Intervening strips that are not pieced are necessary, however, as they reduce the possibility of bumps arising where piecing on neighbouring rows coincides.

- Use a collection of shot, shiny or other textured fabrics whose surfaces look quite different when used for the sloping rows.

- To achieve the look of a Victorian crazy quilt, embroider some of the seams using machine-embroidery stitches.

Special Occasions

What better reason to make a quilt than a special occasion? Here you can enjoy decorating your home for special dates in the calendar by making projects such as the original illuminated Christmas Baubles hanging, or the charming Spring Bunnies quilt for Easter. Celebrate a new arrival in the family or a significant birthday with Love and Kisses in the red-and-white tradition, or recall the holiday of a lifetime with Memento Magic, whose fun pockets can hold those precious reminders. Finally, why not indulge in the delights of Ice-cream Sundae or the Dieters' Dream?

This wall hanging is not, strictly speaking, a quilt. Instead, it consists of sheer fabric to which individually made baubles are attached and behind which there is a net of low-voltage lights. Sheer fabrics are challenging to prepare and machine, so this is not a suitable project for beginners.

Christmas Baubles

APPROXIMATE SIZE OF QUILT

150 x 100 cm (60 x 39 in) – subject to size of net of lights

SEAM ALLOWANCES

0.75 cm (¼ in) unless otherwise stated

YOU WILL NEED

A fabric width of 110–114 cm (43–44 in) unless otherwise stated. Iron all fabrics before cutting.

- Net of lights 150 x 100 cm (60 x 39 in)
- 200 cm (81 in) gold organza (sheer) for the background
- 40 cm (18 in) purple synthetic silk for bauble 1
- 40 cm (18 in) gold metallic fabric for baubles 1 and 2
- 40 cm (18 in) blue metallic fabric for baubles 3 and 6
- 40 cm (18 in) purple metallic fabric for bauble 3
- 40 cm (18 in) red metallic jersey for bauble 4
- 40 cm (18 in) purple satin for bauble 5
- 40 cm (18 in) very pale pink chiffon for bauble 7
- 150 cm (60 in) woven bridal buckram 79 cm (31 in) wide
- 40 cm (18 in) each of lining in colours to suit bauble colours
- 150 cm (60 in) lightweight iron-on interfacing

- 150 cm (60 in) heavy non-woven interfacing
- 100 cm (39 in) thin wadding (batting) 150 cm (60 in) wide
- 150 cm (60 in) fusible webbing
- Strips of tissue paper
- Sew-easy fluid
- Assorted metallic, variegated and shiny machine-embroidery threads
- Assorted lengths of gold ribbon trimmings (maximum 220 cm/90 in length for two baubles)
- Temporary spray adhesive
- Copper piping 15 mm (⅝ in) diameter and 200 cm (81 in) long
- Pipe cutter
- Needles for sewing with metallic threads
- Baking parchment (optional)
- Templates on page 135
- See also Equipment, pages 110–111

NOTE

Referring to the photograph opposite, the baubles are numbered horizontally from top left to bottom right.

Note

It is essential to obtain the lights first and to make the project to fit the lights, rather than the other way around, including deciding which way to hang them to suit your specific location. The lights must be low voltage and remain cool enough to be safe when lit. When attaching them, take care not to pierce the light cable.

> **TIP**
> Tissue or other thin paper strips will assist sewing sheer fabrics: all seams on the sheer background should be sewn with thin paper below to stabilize them. Tear this away after sewing. This stabilizing is absolutely necessary because sheer fabrics are difficult to handle. Clothes pegs can be useful to hold the wires temporarily in place during assembly.

MAKING THE BACKGROUND

Measure the net of lights, because this dictates the dimensions of the hanging (the one here was 150 x 100 cm/59 x 39 in). Consider where you will plug in the transformer: it is heavy and will determine which way the rectangle will be hung (portrait or landscape).

❶ Cut a length of gold organza 160 cm (63 in) plus a top allowance of 10 cm (4 in) for the hanging sleeve and a bottom hem allowance of 10 cm (4 in). This allows both hems to be doubled and gives more substance. Retain the selvedges on the side hems, which will be a scant 3 cm (1¼ in) hem doubled on both sides.

❷ Press the side hems in place and sew. Then press the top and bottom hems and sew.

❸ To make the hanging sleeve, cut a piece of gold organza 13 cm (5 in) deep across the fabric width. Press 0.75 cm (¼ in) twice on both long edges and stitch to form 0.75 cm double hems. Cut into 7 cm (2¾ in) wide pieces and press under narrow double hems. Place along the top of the background, equidistant from one another, and starting 2 cm (¾ in) from each end. Sew to form a sleeve with gaps. This allows you to hook the wires of the light curtain on to the copper pipe in the gaps between the loops (see Assembling the wall hanging, overleaf).

❹ Cut the piping in two to fit the background fabric. The bottom length should be slightly less than the fabric width, for enclosing within the lower hem, while the top should extend beyond the fabric for hanging purposes. (The open ends of the piping allow for suspension hooks to be inserted in the top length to attach the hanging to the wall.) The weight of the piping stabilizes the sheer fabric.

MAKING THE BAUBLES

The following instructions are for making up each complete bauble, including the decorating stage, suggestions for which are shown opposite. It is sensible to make a sample version first. Follow the instructions on Machine-embroidery (see pages 118–119).

❶ Use the template on page 133 to make the shaped bauble. To make a template for the round baubles, draw circles either with a pair of compasses or using a large plate or other circular object. Fold the drawing in half and draw the square-shaped top (**Diagram A**).

❷ For each bauble, using the relevant template and adding 1 cm (³⁄₈ in) seam allowance, cut the fabric, the lining and heavy interfacing. You can back fragile fabrics intended for the bauble fronts with an iron-on interfacing to reduce fraying and to make them easier to sew.

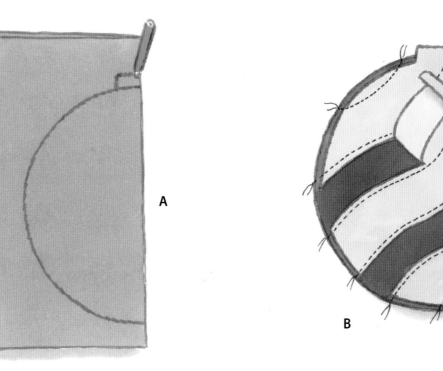

A

B

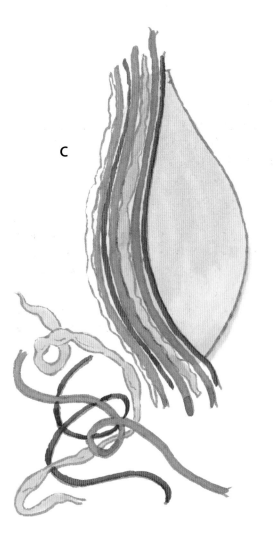

C

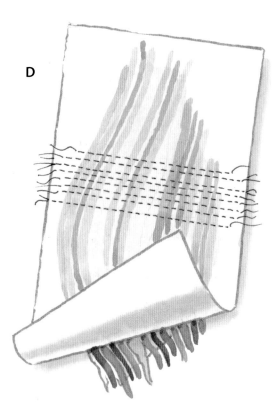

D

3 Decorate the front fabric as desired, or following the suggestions below. Now place the front fabric, right sides together with the lining, and with the interfacing behind the lining, and sew, leaving the square top open for turning right side out. Trim the seam allowances appropriately into layers and snip perpendicularly to the seam. Turn right side out, so the lining is at the back, and press with a cool iron.

4 Use the same templates to cut the bridal buckram, but reduce by 0.75 cm (¼ in) all around. Cut the thin wadding to the same dimension. Stick together using temporary spray adhesive. Roll tightly enough to insert inside the made-up bauble between the interfacing and the lining. Ease flat with care, and press as necessary.

5 Cut a cap for each bauble from scraps of metallic fabric, stiffen and decorate. Choose a short length of ribbon or cord for a hanging loop and sew it to the bauble together with the cap.

DECORATIVE SUGGESTIONS

Baubles 1 and 3 (top left and middle on hanging): To create a counterchange effect, mark the design lines on the top fabric and place the two chosen colours, both right side up, on top. Using a short stitch length, sew along the design lines in a plain thread. Without damaging the layer beneath or the stitching, cut away the top fabric, staying close to the stitching, from alternate sections to reveal the fabric below (**Diagram B**). Choose a suitable braid and couch down to cover the initial stitching.

• Bauble 2 (top right): Use several rows of narrow braid that need only a single line of simple stitching down the centre.

• Baubles 4 and 6 (middle right and bottom left): To decorate with ribbon, fold the front fabric in half horizontally to find a centre line for positioning the lengths of ribbon. Baste in place then machine-sew along both edges using machine-embroidery patterns and decorative threads. Three strips can be enough for good effect.

• Bauble 5 (middle left): Mark a horizontal centre line and from this lightly mark several more straight lines, which can be stitched with decorative thread and fancy stitches. Machine-embroidery lines could alternate with sequin strands or beading.

• Bauble 7 (bottom right): Interface a base fabric (which will not be seen) and cover one side with fusible webbing. Remove the paper then arrange miscellaneous threads and fibres in a swirl on the surface (**Diagram C**). When happy with the appearance, cover with baking parchment (if using) and press to fuse. Place a layer of chiffon over the fused threads and hold all together by parallel rows of straight stitching worked with an interesting thread (**Diagram D**). Complete as above.

ASSEMBLING THE WALL HANGING

❶ The sizes of the baubles partly dictate the layout. Spread out the background layer or hang it temporarily while you decide on a pleasing arrangement for the baubles. Note that some baubles hang in front of the hanging ribbons and cords of others. This determines the order in which they are attached.

❷ Cut a length of ribbon and suspend it over the top sleeve (so that it will take some of the strain when the hanging is upright). Thread the other end through the hanging loop of the bauble, folding it up to secure when sewing to the background. Working each in turn, baste, then sew, the ribbons in position.

❸ Working from the back, lightly baste all the baubles to the background. Check their positions are still satisfactory then hand-sew the baubles to the curtain from the back.

❹ Turn the hanging over and fix the light curtain to the back, hooking the wires over the exposed copper pipe at the top, and bar-tacking the wire to the sides, top and bottom by hand to maintain its position..

Variations

- Making more but smaller baubles would make their placing more flexible. For example, each person in a family could design his or her own bauble decoration, even if not able to carry out the sewing.

- Make a hanging on a themed, printed background without a light curtain. A night sky print could provide a dark ground on which to display light, bright colours well; or a frosted white would make rich deep colours look as if viewed against snow outside a window.

- You could make larger baubles to use as decorations in their own right – perhaps hanging them in a stairwell or against a window. For the latter, you might wish to decorate both sides of each bauble.

Made following the Quilt-as-you-go method (see page 125), this single-bed-sized project uses one of the most traditional colour schemes for quilting – that of red and white. Here, the design is enriched with a range of rosy pinks.

Love and Kisses

APPROXIMATE SIZE OF QUILT
250 x 180 cm (100 x 72 in)
SEAM ALLOWANCES
0.75 cm ('/₄ in) unless otherwise stated

YOU WILL NEED
A fabric width of 110–114 cm (43–44 in) unless otherwise stated. Iron all fabrics before cutting.
- 180 cm (72 in) fine calico for the central blocks
- Two 'fat' quarters (see page 108) red for hearts
- 390 cm (153 in) light pink backing fabric
- 260 cm (102 in) solid or mottled red for binding, sashing and some hearts
- 260 cm (102 in) pink print for back sashing
- 70 cm (27 in) each of three pink print fabrics for border blocks
- 40 cm (18 in) each of three pink print fabrics for border blocks
- 375 cm (144 in) wadding 150 cm (60 in) wide
- 100 cm (39 in) sewable fusible webbing
- Matching sewing threads
- Red machine-embroidery thread for appliqué and quilting
- Invisible thread in smoke or clear
- Baking parchment (optional)
- Templates on page 135
- See also Equipment, pages 110–111

CUTTING

❶ From the calico, cut fifteen 31.5 x 31.5 cm (12½ x 12½ in) squares.

❷ From the backing fabric, cut thirty-five 31.5 x 31.5 cm (12½ x 12½ in) squares.

❸ From the red fabric, cut two 260 x 11.5 cm (102 x 4½ in) strips and two 190 x 11.5 cm (74 x 4½ in) strips for binding. Also, cut four 260 x 6.5 cm (102 x 2½ in) strips and thirty 33 x 6.5 cm (13 x 2½ in) strips for sashing the top of the quilt.

❹ From the back sashing fabric, cut four 260 x 5.75 cm (102 x 2¼ in) strips and thirty 33 x 5.75 cm (13 x 2¼ in).

❺ From the assorted pinks, cut twenty 31.5 x 31.5 cm (12½ x 12½in) squares for the border blocks. From the 40 cm (18 in) lengths you can cut two blocks each. The longer lengths can give four to six blocks.

❻ Cut the wadding into fifteen 35 x 35 cm (14 x 14 in) squares; sixteen 35 x 40 cm (14 x 16 in) rectangles; four 40 x 40 cm (16 x 16 in) squares.

Note
The back sashing strips are intentionally narrower than those for the front so that any stitching is covered by the front sashings. The wadding sizes are larger than the fabric squares so that the sashing strips are filled, too, and to allow for slight trimming to square up later, if necessary. If the quantities for the sashing look rather large, this is because the intention is to cut the long sashings as entire strips. If you do not mind joins, you could allow less fabric to save money.

MAKING THE APPLIQUÉ BLOCKS

❶ Choose which of the many heart-shaped templates on page 135 you wish to use, or draw your own. Follow the instructions for Appliqué techniques (see pages 116–117) to trace the templates and fuse the cut shapes on to the wrong side of your chosen fabric. Then bond the hearts on to the right side of eight of the calico squares. Be free with the placement angles, but try to keep each heart centred on its square.

❷ Make up a 'sandwich' of a heart-calico square, right side up, small wadding square and backing square, right side down. Ensure the fabric squares are centred above and below the wadding, which will protrude all around (**Diagram A**), then pin or baste the 'sandwich' to hold the layers in place.

❸ Set up your machine and work a small test on scraps of all three layers before working the blocks. Have bobbin thread to blend with the light pink backing and machine-embroidery thread of your choice on top. Working through all the layers, satin-stitch or zigzag-stitch around the heart, starting at the top centre dip in the heart. When you near the bottom point of the heart, narrow the stitch width, if possible, then gradually return the stitch width back to its original setting once you have turned the point.

❹ Repeat the process to complete the eight heart-calico blocks.

MAKING THE 'KISS' BLOCKS

❶ Seven calico squares for the quilt centre and 20 pink squares for the border need to be marked as follows. Without stretching, lightly crease each fabric square diagonally both ways. Pencil a fine line 2.5 cm (1 in) from the diagonal on all four sides to make a 5 cm (2 in) wide 'kiss' across the square. Alternatively, carefully position 5 cm (2 in) wide masking tape centred over the two diagonals.

❷ Layer each marked calico square as for the heart-calico squares. For the pink corner border squares, use the large squares of wadding and layer up in an offset position, as shown in **Diagram B**. For the pink border side squares, use the rectangles of wadding and offset the fabric as shown in **Diagram C**. These different positions ensure that a border of wadding is left at the edge of the quilt for filling the binding when you finish the quilt. Note that the top and backing squares must still be accurately aligned on either side of the wadding. Pin or baste, avoiding the markings, to hold the three layers securely together.

❸ Follow the instructions for Machine-quilting (see page 123) to quilt the blocks. Wind the bobbin to match the machine-embroidery thread of your choice on top. If your machine has a 'hand-quilting' stitch, or you have a fancy stitch you particularly like, now is the time to use it. Machine-quilt the outline of each 'kiss'. Trim the wadding if necessary.

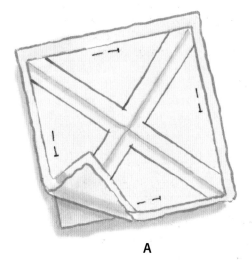

A

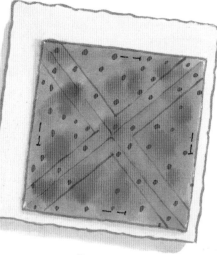

B

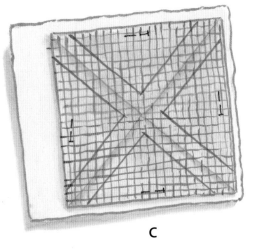

C

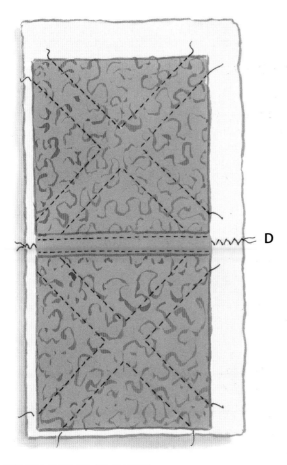

D

ASSEMBLING THE QUILT

❶ Prepare the sashing. Press 0.75 cm (¹⁄₄ in) turnings to the wrong side on the long edges only of all the print sashing strips for the quilt back. Repeat for the red sashing strips for the quilt front.

❷ Lay the blocks out on a bed or the floor in a five-by-seven grid. Starting with the left-hand border row, select the top corner block and the block immediately below it, and butt the two wadding squares together. Sew the wadding only, matching the thread to the back sashing print and using a fairly wide zigzag stitch.

❸ When joined, position a back sashing strip in place, covering the raw edges of both backing squares by 0.5 cm (scant ¹⁄₄ in) and noting that the strip is not intended to extend fully to the top and bottom edges of the wadding. Pin, ensuring that the front blocks are securely in place. Straight-stitch both edges of the sashing strip through all layers (**Diagram D**).

❹ Turn the two joined blocks right side up and pin the red front sashing strip in place, to cover the stitching lines where the back

sashing was attached. Change the top thread to the invisible thread and select the blind-hem stitch on your machine. Blind-hem-stitch the strip into place on both edges.

❺ Now add the next block in the sequence in the same way and repeat the process until you have five long columns of blocks. To save changing thread quite so often during the process, repeat each step for each column of blocks before moving to the next step.

❻ Join the columns of blocks together in the correct order, as above.

FINISHING

For this project, the binding is attached to each side of the quilt separately to mirror the look of the sashing.

❶ The wide binding includes a 0.75 cm (¹⁄₄ in) turning allowance on the long sides of the strip. Press these before sewing the strips to the quilt.

❷ Use machine-sewing stitch to sew the first long binding strip, right sides together, down one long side of the back of the quilt. Fold the binding to the front of the quilt, bringing the turned edge to cover the existing stitching and pin (the wadding should fill the binding). Change to invisible thread on the top of the machine and blind-hem into place, then trim the excess fabric.

❸ Repeat this on the opposite long side of the quilt, then on the top and bottom short edges of the quilt, where the ends must also be folded neatly to enclose the raw edges. Change the bobbin thread to red for the border portion and edge, then to light pink for the body of the quilt so that the stitches blend into the tonal backgrounds.

❹ Label the quilt (see page 129) to finish.

Variations

- Adapt the construction method to make quilts of different sizes, such as a five-by-five lap size, or a seven-by-seven double-bed size.
- Instead of using the same decorative stitch for machine-quilting all of the blocks, use a different stitch pattern or thread for each.

The intention with this kitchen wall hanging was to create cakes in fabric that looked good enough to eat. They are made as individual items, using a method devised by British quilter Linda Straw. As with block patchwork, any unsuccessful attempts can be discarded without affecting the final quilt.

Dieters' Dream

APPROXIMATE SIZE OF QUILT

75 x 76 cm (29½ x 30 in)

SEAM ALLOWANCES

0.75 cm (¼ in) unless otherwise stated

YOU WILL NEED

A fabric width of 110–114 cm (43–44 in) unless otherwise stated. Iron all fabrics before cutting.

- Eight 'fat' eighths of cake-coloured fabrics
- Seven to nine 25 cm (10 in) squares of 'icing' fabrics, including chocolate
- Three 25 cm (10 in) squares of 'plate' fabrics
- Assorted scraps for cake details: red satin, brown metallic fabric, cream chiffon
- 225 cm (90 in) grey 'cracked ice' or wood-grain fabric, for the shelf unit
- 90 cm (36 in) low-loft wadding (batting) for entire unit, plus scraps for individual cakes
- 150 cm (60 in) lightweight non-woven, non-fusible interfacing 90 cm (36 in) wide
- 20 cm (9 in) firm interfacing
- Embellishments as desired: beaded trims, lace doilies, embroidered edgings
- Assorted machine-embroidery threads
- Sewing thread to match shelf fabric
- Templates on page 136–137
- See also Equipment, pages 110–111

CUTTING

❶ From the grey fabric, cut two 66.5 x 32 cm (26 x 12½ in) rectangles, and label that the reverse side is to be decorated with the cakes.

❷ Also from the grey fabric, cut two 79 x 18 cm (31 x 7 in) rectangles for the pediment. Cut a strip of wadding and a strip of firm interfacing to the same size.

❸ Also from the grey fabric, cut one 66.5 x 4 cm (26 x 1½ in) strip for the top shelf edge; one 66.5 x 7 cm (26 x 2¾ in) strip for the lower shelf edge; four 62 x 6.5 cm (24½ x 2½ in) strips for the side frame and side binding; and one 78 x 6.5 cm (31 x 2½ in) for the lower binding.

❹ Set the remaining grey fabric aside for cutting the backing and hanging sleeves later.

MAKING A CAKE

Read the advice on Machine-embroidery (see pages 118–119) before starting. Instructions follow for the simple sponge cake, to the top left of the wall hanging. It is advisable to make a sample first.

❶ Copy the cake pattern from page 137 to full size and reverse it simply by turning it over and tracing the outline using a dark pen.

❷ Place a rectangle of lightweight interfacing over the reversed cake pattern and trace. This is the side from which you will sew first. Turn this drawn side down and lay a piece of thin wadding on top, followed by a light-coloured 'icing' fabric, right side up, and a textured 'cake' fabric, also right side up. Flip the drawn side back to the top and pin a few times through all the layers, making sure you avoid any drawn lines.

❸ Load the machine with suitable thread (dark enough for you to see the stitching on the front side, since you need to follow it later). You can either free-machine with your work in an embroidery hoop, or just sew steadily with the embroidery foot and a short stitch length. Sew over the whole of your drawn outline (**Diagram A**). Every shape should be enclosed by a line.

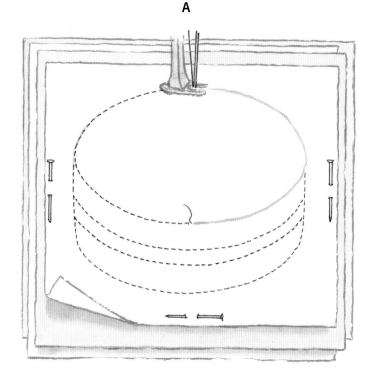

A

❹ Turn the work right side up. Very carefully, cut away the 'cake' fabric from where it covers the 'icing' on the top of the cake and around the filling (**Diagram B**). Cut close to the stitching without damaging it or the fabric. To help separate the layers, use a pin to pick up a tiny amount of the top fabric only. When you can feel it lifting the two layers apart, snip the pin free, leaving a small hole for inserting the tip of your scissors.

❺ With the embroidery foot in place, select a thread colour for the final embroidery and zigzag- or satin-stitch around the outlines, swinging wide enough to completely cover the remaining trimmed fabric. (The stitch length need not be short enough to obliterate the previous stitching on this first pass because the cake will be sewn around again later.) Cut the cake out, again very close to the stitching.

❻ Most cakes need just two layers of fabric but a few need three (the Battenberg, éclairs, jam tarts and the cake on a pedestal plate). Repeat the process above for the first two layers and trim to reveal the lighter layer. Then position a piece of the stronger colour (red satin for jam or dark brown metallic fabric for chocolate), a little larger than the area it needs to cover, right side up, and turn to the back to sew the relevant enclosed shape, possibly along a line already stitched. Turn the work over and trim away excess from the new shape. In this way, almost any number of shapes in different colours and fabrics can be attached. Do not begin to zigzag- or satin-stitch until all the fabrics have been attached.

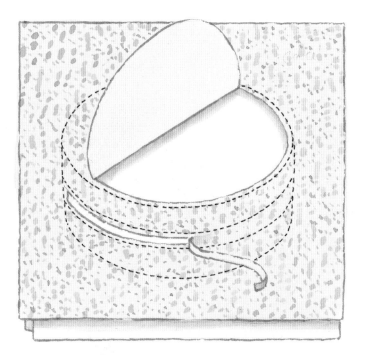

B

CAKE EMBELLISHMENTS

Further details can now be added:

7 Make small, scattered hand-stitches (known as seeding) with multi-coloured thread to resemble candy cake decorations.

8 Work lines of quilting by hand or machine to imitate ripples or swirls in the icing, as seen on the Swiss roll.

9 The piped cream in the cream horns begins as a circle of light fabric. Insert a row of running stitches or long machine stitches around the edge and gather it up to fit the end of the horn. Sew in place, turning in the raw edge. Then, with small stitches, gradually fasten down the excess fabric into ripples and swirls (**Diagram C**).

10 The look of a piped edge of icing or cream can be achieved by taking a narrow strip of chiffon, folding the long sides to the middle and working a zigzag line of hand running-stitch down its length (**Diagram D**). When gathered, this will look like piping and can be sewn to cover a single-sewn edge. However, this type of three-dimensional trim is best added once the cake has been sewn to the shelf background because it can get in the way of machining around the cake. Similarly, attach purchased trims after attaching cakes to background shelf.

C

D

MAKING THE SHELF UNIT

1 Spread out the two large grey fabric rectangles, wrong side up, and arrange your cakes on them. Having some cakes in front of others helps give the illusion of depth, but do not feel too tied to reality. You may want to add a lace doily (or part of one) below some cakes. When you are happy with the arrangement, sew the cakes in place with a final pass of zigzag or satin stitching, neatening the edge and covering any remaining straight stitching. Keep the outer edge of any doilies unattached to fold out of the way for the next step.

2 Machine-sew the appropriate shelf-edge strip to the lower edge of the top shelf. Repeat for the bottom shelf, including a length of embroidered trimming, if desired. Press both shelf units then sew them together. Next sew the wide side strips to the sides.

3 Now cut a rectangle of backing from the remaining grey fabric, slightly larger than the quilt top, and layer both together with the low-loft wadding (see Assembling the quilt top, pages 120–121). Machine-quilt around the shelf rectangles, without crossing any cakes.

4 Attach the remaining side strips to the sides as a binding, finishing 1.5 cm (⅝ in) wide. Turn in the raw edge on the back and hand-sew to finish. (Here, they were worked with the back of the fabric showing, like the shelf unit interior.)

5 Attach the bottom binding strip, right side out, and finish as above.

6 Copy the pediment shape from the template on to the wrong side of one of the pediment rectangles. Sew two narrow pin tucks, the first 7 cm (2¾ in) down from the top corner on the right side and the second 1.25 cm (½ in) below on the wrong side. Press.

7 Layer together the marked rectangle, drawn side up, right sides together with the second backing rectangle (which will now be slightly longer), plus the rectangles of firm interfacing and wadding. Sew around the shape, starting along one short end, going across the shaped top and down the second short end. Trim the seam allowances into layers, removing as much as possible of the wadding and interfacing. Clip into the curves then turn right side out and press. Quilt through all the layers 1.5 cm (⅝ in) from the shaped top edge.

8 Keeping the backing layer free, place right sides together with the shelf unit and sew through all the layers. Again, trim the wadding and interfacing close to the seam. Fold the pediment right side up and press. On the back, fold in the raw edge and hand sew.

9 Make a hanging sleeve (in two parts, if wished) and add a label (see page 129) to finish.

Variations

- Replace the grey shelf fabric and adjust the proportions of the shelf unit to suit your kitchen. Shape the pediment at the top to imitate furniture that you own.

- Use the cake motifs to produce a set of place mats – each family member choosing his or her favourite. Avoid using very three-dimensional details if you intend to put plates on them.

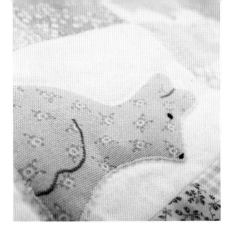

The success of this fresh, pretty quilt lies in the fact that it draws on an extensive collection of harmonious fabric scraps. Use fewer fabrics to make the cutting out quicker – especially for the four-patch setting blocks – and machine-quilt the long diagonals if you prefer.

Spring Bunnies

APPROXIMATE SIZE OF QUILT
182 x 132.5 cm (71 x 53 in)

SEAM ALLOWANCES
0.75 cm (¼ in) unless otherwise stated

YOU WILL NEED
A fabric width of 110–114 cm (43–44 in) unless otherwise stated. Iron all fabrics before cutting.
- 140 cm (54 in) unbleached calico (muslin) for the large blocks
- 21 x 30 cm (8¼ x 12 in) pieces of approximately 41 different fabrics (small prints, checks and polka dots) for the setting blocks and appliquéd bunnies
- 190 cm (72 in) aquamarine print for borders and binding
- 290 cm (117 in) backing fabric
- 150 cm (60 in) sewable fusible webbing
- 200 cm (81 in) wadding (batting) 150 cm (60 in) wide
- Neutral sewing thread and a few colours for sewing details
- Pigma pen (or embroidery thread) for eyes and noses
- Templates on page 137
- See also Equipment, pages 110–111

CUTTING

1 From the unbleached calico, cut forty-one 19.5 x 14 cm (7½ x 5½ in) rectangles.

2 From each 21 x 30 cm (8¼ x 12 in) rectangle of scrap fabric, cut four 10.5 x 7.75 cm (4 x 3 in) patches.

3 From the aquamarine print, working parallel to one selvedge to avoid the need for joins, cut border strips as follows: two 170 x 11.5 cm (67 x 4½ in) strips and two 140 x 11.5 cm (55 x 4½ in) strips. From the remainder cut 6.75 cm (2½ in) wide strips to total 655 cm (260 in) when joined for binding.

4 Divide the backing fabric in half and seam together to make up the necessary area with the seam running horizontally (see Backing fabric, page 122).

APPLIQUÉING THE BUNNIES

1 From what remains of the scrap fabric, and following the instructions for Appliqué techniques (see pages 116–117), cut 17 large bunnies facing in each direction (a total of 34) and seven small bunnies facing in each direction (a total of 14) from the templates on page 137. Fuse the large bunnies to 34 of the calico blocks, taking care to have them sitting straight. Fuse two small bunnies to each of the seven remaining calico blocks, one facing each way per block.

2 In the same way, and using what remains of the calico, cut six small bunnies facing in each direction for the border (a total of 12). Fuse the small calico bunnies to the top and bottom borders, three facing away from the centre on each side.

3 Load a neutral thread in the machine and zigzag- or satin-stitch around all the bunnies, starting between the ears at the top on the large ones and starting in the notch under the chin of the small ones (**Diagram A**).

4 To work the stitched detail of haunches and ears on the large bunnies, use the hatched area on the template to draw a pencil line for the haunch and follow the dotted line for the ear line. Sort into basic colour families and sew the details on all in each colour family with a single shade of thread.

5 Add eyes to all the bunnies and noses to the large ones with a Pigma pen (or embroider them if you wish).

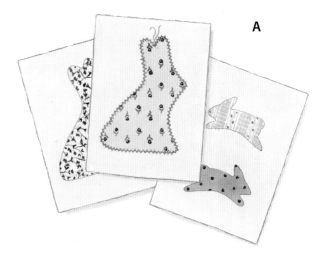

A

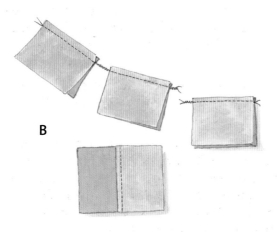

B

MAKING THE FOUR-PATCH SETTING BLOCKS

1 Sort the patches into pairs that look good together. Follow the instructions on Patchwork techniques (see pages 114–115) to sew one of each pair together, chaining from one to the next (**Diagram B**), and pressing the seams towards the darker fabric.

2 Now sew the two corresponding pairs together in a counterchange pattern to complete the 19.5 x 14 cm (7½ x 5½ in) block. Press seams.

ASSEMBLING THE QUILT TOP

1 Starting with a large bunny appliqué block, lay out the bunny blocks alternating with the pieced four-patch blocks in nine rows of nine blocks (**Diagram C**). Note where to place the seven blocks of tiny bunnies. Rearrange until you are satisfied.

2 Follow the instructions on Assembling the quilt top (see pages 120–121) to sew the blocks together in rows, pressing the seams in neighbouring rows in opposite directions.

3 Sew the rows together and then press the seams towards the top of the quilt.

4 Follow the instructions for Attaching borders (see page 121) to sew on the side borders first. Press, then attach the top and bottom borders, press and trim.

C

QUILTING AND FINISHING

❶ Follow the instructions for Traditional quilting (see page 122) to layer up the top, wadding and backing.

❷ Quilt the long diagonals through the four-patch blocks first to stabilize the work. Quilt by machine or by hand, if preferred.

❸ Quilt around the bunnies, either outlining them by hand close to the appliqué (as here), or echoing the shape farther away, for example, 0.75 cm (¼ in).

❹ In the border, besides quilting around the tiny bunnies, add little curving 'hops' from one to the next. Use masking tape parallel to the seam to quilt a frame around the remaining border (**Diagram C**). Add a further line if wished.

❺ Follow the instructions for Binding (see pages 126–128) to finish the quilt. This binding finishes to 1.75 cm (¾ in). Sew it on 2 cm (¾ in) from the quilt edge, press to the back of the quilt and turn in 0.75 cm (¼ in) to hem in place.

❻ Label the quilt (see page 129) to finish.

Variations

• Resize the quilt, either adding more rows of setting blocks or removing some. The large bunnies could face in opposite directions on alternate rows, or you could omit the small-bunny blocks altogether to suit your revised plan.

• Make the quilt using non-pieced setting blocks. You will need 140 cm (54 in) fabric, cut into 19.5 x 14 cm (7½ x 5½ in) blocks.

• Use the Quilt-as-you-go method to construct the quilt (see page 125). Start by joining blocks into rows, as above, then follow the instructions to sew the rows on to the basted backing and wadding, working from the centre row of blocks outwards. Add the borders in a similar manner, and finish as above.

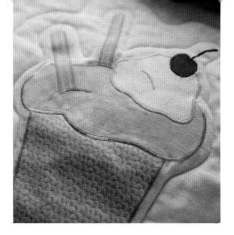

This quilt is actually a 'quillow', having a pocket on the backing into which the whole quilt can be folded, either for easy carriage or for use as a cushion. It is a lap-size quilt but could easily fit a child's bed. Hand-dyed cottons were used for the block backgrounds but similar fabrics are available commercially.

Ice-cream Sundae

APPROXIMATE SIZE OF QUILT
145 x 122 cm (57 x 48 in)
SEAM ALLOWANCES
0.75 cm (¼ in) unless otherwise stated

YOU WILL NEED
A fabric width of 110–114 cm (43–44 in) unless otherwise stated. Iron all fabrics before cutting.
- Ten 'fat' quarters (see page 108) of ice-cream colours for block backgrounds and pocket
- A handful of scraps for appliqué details
- Five 'fat' quarters of biscuit-coloured prints for sashing and strip-piecing
- 70 cm (27 in) biscuit-coloured print for binding
- 275 cm (108 in) backing fabric
- 100 cm (39 in) fusible webbing
- Scrap of fusible interfacing (optional)
- 140 cm (54 in) wadding (batting)
- Beige sewing thread
- Machine-embroidery threads in ice-cream colours for appliqué
- Templates on pages 138–139
- See also Equipment, pages 110–111

CUTTING

1 From the ice-cream-coloured fabrics, cut the following rectangles: five at 42 x 31.5 cm (16½ x 12½ in) (block A); two at 37 x 31.5 cm (14½ x 12½ in) (block B); one at 32 x 31.5 cm (12½ x 12½ in) (block C); two at 27 x 31.5 cm (10½ x 12½ in) (block D). Keep the leftover scraps for use in the long sashings.

2 From the biscuit-coloured fabrics (and any remaining binding fabric, see below), cut two 5.5 cm (2 in) wide strips for the long sashings. Then, from each fabric, cut a few strips of random width not less than 4 cm (1½ in) and not greater than 6.5 cm (2½ in) for the horizontal sashings. More strips of either can be cut later as needed.

3 From the binding fabric, cut 5.5 cm (2 in) wide strips to total 560 cm (220 in) when joined.

MAKING THE APPLIQUÉ BLOCKS

❶ Follow the instructions on Appliqué techniques (see pages 116–117) to work the appliqué blocks. Templates are given for the sundae dishes, cornet and lollipop, but feel free to improvise, especially with details such as the finger wafers and fruits. Scoops of ice cream are easily cut as simple circles.

❷ Finish the blocks with machine-embroidery using threads such as the shaded pink used to add the illusion of depth to the shapes (see page 69). For fine details such as the cherry stalk, which has stitching without a fabric shape, iron a scrap of fusible interfacing behind where you intend to sew.

ASSEMBLING THE QUILT TOP

❶ Lay the blocks out into rows following the plan shown in **Diagram A**. (One B block has been retained for the pocket.)

❷ To make the horizontal sashing, sew together two sets of the random-width biscuit-coloured strips, joining the long edges together, to measure at least 31.5 cm (12½ in) across. Press all the seams the same way. From these sets, cut six slices 31.5 x 14 cm (12½ x 5½ in).

❸ Place the horizontal sashing between the blocks, rotating some for more variety, and follow the instructions for Joining blocks with sashing (see page 121) to sew the blocks and sashing together to form three columns. Measure the column length.

A

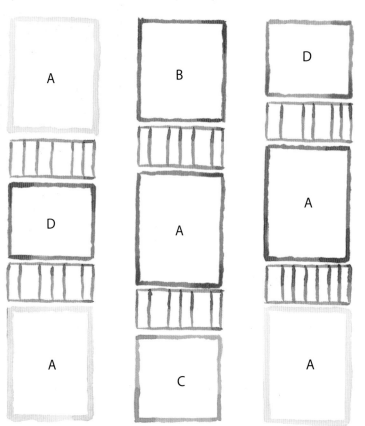

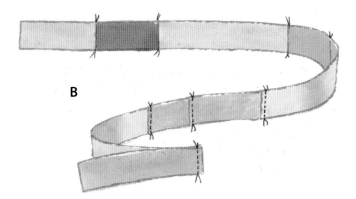

B

❹ Using the 5.5 cm (2 in) wide biscuit-coloured strips, interspersed with short leftovers from the block backgrounds or other scraps – also cut to this width – piece together eight strips to match the row length (**Diagram B**). Sew these strips together in pairs and press.

❺ Place two of these sets between the rows and join together. Then add the remaining two pairs of strips to the outer edges. Press, then measure the quilt width.

❻ Repeat step 4 to make four more 5.5 cm (2 in) wide strips pieced from biscuit-coloured fabrics and other scraps as you like. Join the strips into pairs to equal the quilt width. Press and sew to the top and bottom edges to complete the quilt top.

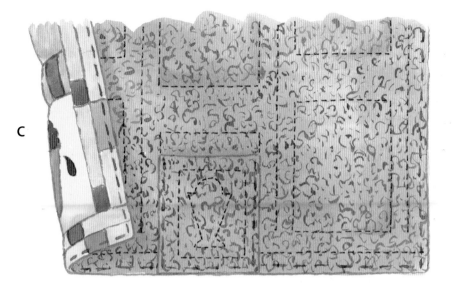

C

QUILTING AND FINISHING

❶ Divide the backing fabric into two equal lengths. Join these together, pressing the seam open. With the seam horizontal, measure off 155 cm (61 in) for the backing and trim. From the excess, cut a square 47 x 47 cm (18½ x 18½ in) for the quillow pocket.

❷ Follow the directions for Quilting techniques (see pages 122–123) to layer up the backing, wadding and quilt top.

❸ Machine-quilt around the blocks, then along the seam in the middle of the long sashing. If wished, also quilt a simplified outline or two around the appliqué shapes.

❹ Follow the instructions for Binding (see page 126) to prepare the quilt edges for finishing, trimming as necessary and basting.

❺ Use the leftover biscuit fabrics to frame the remaining appliqué block, bringing it up to 47 x 47 cm (18½ x 18½ in). Place the block right side down on the same-size backing square and sew on three sides, leaving the bottom of the pocket open. Turn right side out and press carefully. Machine-sew around the frame and around the motif to hold the layers together.

❻ Position the pocket on the back of the quilt, centred along the lower edge, with raw edges level and with the right side down. Baste along the two sides and at the quilt edge (**Diagram C**).

❼ Now bind the quilt (see pages 126–127) and hand-sew the edges of the pocket to the backing without coming through to the quilt front. Add a label to the back of the quilt (see page 129).

PACKING

❶ To pack the quilt inside its pocket, have the quilt right side up and fold in the two long sides to align with the pocket sides.

❷ Now fold the top of the quilt down in thirds. The resulting rectangle should now fit inside when the pocket is turned right side out.

Variations

- Keep the colour scheme but use the cake motifs from Dieters' Dream (see pages 58–63). Adapt the block sizes if necessary, maybe using more blocks of the smaller size with more, but narrower, horizontal sashing strips.

- If short of materials, the pocket could be scrap-pieced.

- Replace the pastel colours with various rich dark browns and some creams to produce a chocolate ice-cream sundae.

This type of folded construction makes the most of shiny or shot fabrics. Careful preparation is important when working with several layers of fabric, but it is their volume that maximizes the sheen of the fabrics as the light falls upon them.

Memento Magic

APPROXIMATE SIZE OF QUILT

80 x 60 cm (32 x 24 in)

SEAM ALLOWANCES

0.75 cm (¼ in) unless otherwise stated

YOU WILL NEED

A fabric width of 110–114 cm (43–44 in) unless otherwise stated. Iron all fabrics before cutting.

- 14 'fat' eighths (see page 108) of metallic/shot fabrics
- 100 cm (39 in) striped metallic fabric for borders and binding
- 90 cm (36 in) backing fabric
- 90 cm (36 in) low-loft wadding (batting)
- Dark sewing thread
- Invisible thread in smoke
- See also Equipment, pages 110–111

CUTTING

❶ Sort the fat eighths into two sets: one for the block backgrounds and the other for the triangles. (Either group can include the stripe chosen for the borders.)

❷ From the background set, cut 11.5 x 11.5 cm (4½ x 4½ in) squares. A total of 24 is needed for the quilt centre, plus two for the border.

❸ From the set for the triangles, cut 10 x 10 cm (4 x 4 in) squares. A total of 48 is needed for the centre, plus four for the border. (It is sensible to cut two of each of the fabrics in the set to experiment with combinations before cutting the remainder.)

❹ From the striped metallic fabric, and planning how you wish to use the stripe, cut the border strips as follows: two 66 x 11.5 cm (26 x 4½ in) strips for the top and bottom borders; two 42 x 11.5 cm (17 x 4½ in) strips for the side borders and two 11.5 x 11.5 cm (4½ x 4½ in) squares, also for the side borders. All the borders are a little oversize to allow for trimming.

❺ From the remaining striped metallic fabric cut bias strips 4 cm (1½ in) wide totalling 300 cm (120 in) for binding when joined.

MAKING THE POCKET BLOCKS

1 Fold the smaller squares diagonally into triangles, then, with a cool iron and no steam, press them carefully without stretching the bias fold.

2 Spread out the larger squares in six rows of four and compose a pleasing arrangement. Place two folded triangles on the two lower corners, aligning the raw edges. You may prefer always to have the right or left triangle on top, though in this quilt it is varied. Cut more triangles as necessary to fill all the blocks. Stand back to consider the positioning of the light-coloured fabrics especially.

3 When you are happy with the arrangement, baste the two triangles to each background square with running stitch in the seam allowance where it need not be removed, and return each to its correct place (**Diagram A**). Do not skip the basting, as it prevents the layers from moving as you proceed.

4 Follow the instructions for Assembling the quilt top (see pages 120–121) to join the pocket blocks. Place the first two in the top row right sides together, matching the appropriate raw edges and corners carefully, and pin or thread-baste across the seam. Using a suitable dark thread colour, machine-sew the two blocks together. There are more layers than usual, six for most of every seam, so run the machine slowly. Press the seam open to spread the volume of the seam allowances.

5 Continue the process to join all the blocks into horizontal rows. When joining the rows together, match up the vertical seams carefully, pinning through the seam allowances to keep them open as you sew. Press these seams towards the bottom of the quilt.

6 For the pocket blocks in the side borders, compose and baste two more blocks.

ASSEMBLING THE QUILT

1 Follow the directions for Quilt-as-you-go (see page 125) to prepare a rectangle each of backing and wadding.

2 Centre the assembled blocks and baste into place thoroughly on all sides. Machine-quilt along the vertical and horizontal seams.

3 Assemble the side border strips as follows: sew the right-hand side with a square at the top, then the pocket block, then a side

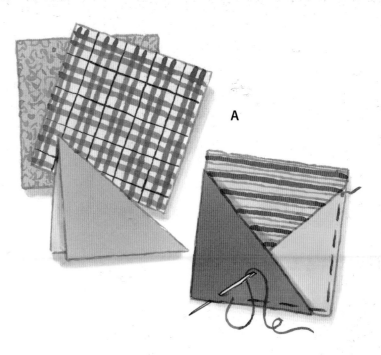

A

border strip; sew the left-hand border with a square at the bottom, then a pocket block, then a side border strip.

4 Using the 'flip and sew' method described in Steamers Ahoy! (see pages 14–17), attach the side borders. Then, in the same manner, add the top and bottom borders.

5 Follow the directions for Double binding (see pages 126–128) to prepare the quilt edges, and bind to finish 0.75 cm (¼ in) wide.

6 Make a hanging sleeve from leftover backing fabric, if wished, and label (see page 129) to finish.

Variations

- If the folded bias edges of the triangles seem stretchy, and the contents likely to fall out, catch the two triangles together with a button or bead or other embellishment.

- Adapt to use as an advent quilt by using suitably themed fabrics and omitting the pocket blocks in the borders. (Instead, make plain side borders to the same size as the top and bottom borders.) The 24 pockets could contain tiny surprises to be opened each day.

Modern Quilts

The projects in this chapter go some way beyond working a conventional quilt top. Two projects, Coffee and Cream and Take A Bite, involve a strip-pieced, quilt-as-you-go construction, which is then developed by cutting and reassembly. Cutting into the quilt is also required for the Enchanted Forest, where it provides interactive play opportunities with toys or puppets. The three remaining projects explore the joys of surface texture: Winter Wonderland with delicate machine-embroidered images, Spencer's Sunflowers with naive three-dimensional blooms and Bright Kites – which scarcely seem attached to their quilted sky!

This project uses the reduced Fibonacci series, a mathematical progression of numbers, to determine the widths of strip to be cut. The monochrome colour scheme draws attention to the quilt's surface, with the interplay of light and shade falling upon the various fabrics sewn, cut and rearranged.

Coffee and Cream

APPROXIMATE SIZE OF QUILT

142 x 108 cm (56 x 42½ in)

SEAM ALLOWANCES

0.75 cm (¼ in) unless stated otherwise

YOU WILL NEED

A fabric width of 110–114 cm (43–44 in) unless otherwise stated. Iron all fabrics before cutting.

- 160 cm (63 in) nut-brown silk for strip-piecing and binding
- Six assorted cream fabrics for strip-piecing, minimum 10 cm (4 in) maximum 30 cm (12 in)
- 220 cm (86 in) backing fabric
- 190 cm (75 in) wadding (batting)
- Sewing thread to match light range
- Invisible thread
- Perle thread or similar in cream colour for ties
- 115 cm (45 in) lightest weight interfacing (optional, see Tip)
- See also Equipment, pages 110–111

CUTTING

❶ From the nut-brown silk, and working across the fabric from selvedge to selvedge, follow the cutting chart in **Diagram A** (overleaf) to cut the appropriate-width strips (which include 1.5 cm/½ in for seam allowances). Number the pieces and stack them in the correct order, working from the left.

❷ From the remaining nut-brown silk, cut 7.5 cm (3 in) wide strips to total 530 cm (210 in) binding when joined.

❸ To cut the assorted cream fabrics, first decide which fabric to use for which strip in the design, then follow the chart to cut the appropriate-width strips (which include 1.5 cm/½ in for seam allowances). Label each strip as you cut it and stack in the correct order as before.

❹ From the backing fabric, cut a piece 175 cm (69 in) long. The remainder will be used to finish the seams on the back.

> **TIP**
> Choose your cream-coloured fabrics carefully. Brocade may be expensive and therefore you may wish to use it for a narrow strip. If you can decide which fabric goes where before buying, you can buy just enough for each strip in multiples of 10 cm (4 in). If any fabric is particularly 'wriggly', iron it to a matching sized length of interfacing to stabilize it.

A

4 cm (1½ in)	9 cm (3½ in)	21.5 cm (8½ in)	9 cm (3½ in)	4 cm (1½ in)	24 cm (9½ in)	21.5 cm (8½ in)

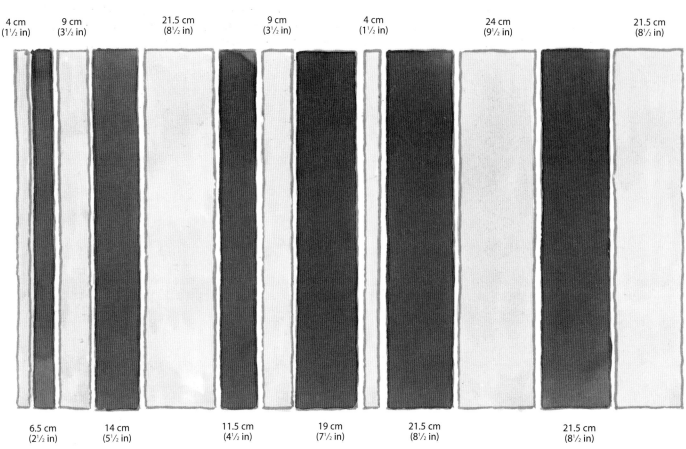

6.5 cm (2½ in)	14 cm (5½ in)	11.5 cm (4½ in)	19 cm (7½ in)	21.5 cm (8½ in)	21.5 cm (8½ in)

ASSEMBLING THE QUILT

1 Follow the instructions for Quilt-as-you-go (see page 125) to layer together the rectangle of backing with the wadding, and thread-baste lengthwise at intervals of 10–15 cm (4–6 in).

2 Position the first narrow cream strip along one short edge of the wadding and thread-baste the first edge within the seam allowance. You may wish to fold the edge of the backing fabric over this raw edge to reduce fraying while working. Take care to get this first strip absolutely straight. Pin or thread-baste the other edge to which the next strip will be attached.

3 Position the second strip (nut-brown silk), right side down, over the first. Pin or thread-baste, then sew carefully through all the layers. Flip the second strip right side up and lightly press.

4 Following the cutting chart above, repeat the process to attach all the strips. Thread-baste the outer edge of the last strip. Always check when sewing a light strip on to a dark one that the dark seam allowance does not project beyond the light one to be visible through the quilt surface. If necessary, trim the dark one carefully.

5 On the wider strips, use invisible thread to add one or two lines of machine-quilting parallel to the seams. If wished, scatter a few ties of perle thread to hold a broad strip to the background, as used on this quilt with the embroidered silk.

6 Spread the quilt out, right side up, on a flat surface and fold the lower left-hand end up to meet the top edge (see Fold A in **Diagram B**). Lightly press with your fingers to mark a crease then unfold. Mark a straight line along the crease and insert a line of thread-basting on each side of this line. Now cut along the line carefully.

7 Place the basted edge of the cut triangle, right side down, along the top edge of the remaining quilt with raw edges level. Pin, thread-baste, then sew. Lightly press the seam open. Trim some of the wadding from between the layers, if possible, for a flatter finish.

8 Now measure Edge C (**Diagram C**) to find out where to cut the lower right-hand corner off (at Line B in **Diagram C**) for attaching to the top right of the new shape. Fold and press a crease, then mark and thread-baste on either side of the line. Cut and attach this triangle as above.

9 The quilt may now need to be trimmed into an even rectangle. Thread-baste any outer edges that are not yet secured. Pay special attention to the lower edge, which is on the bias: insert a line of hand-basting within the seam allowance to avoid it stretching during binding.

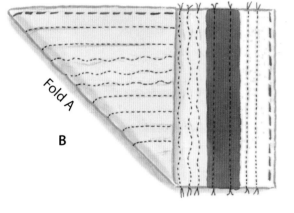

Fold A

B

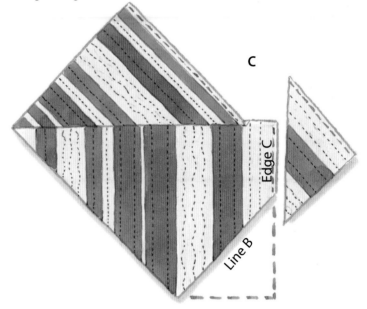

C

Edge C

Line B

Variations

- If you cannot find sufficient differently textured fabrics in the cream value, try reversing the idea to use a single cream silk and six mixed darks.

- Any pairing of colours would work well: consider light grey with shades of old gold, or cream with a range of deep reds or purples.

- Having pieced the quilt-as-you-go rectangle, bind the quilt to finish without cutting and reassembling it. You would need to cut a little more binding.

FINISHING

1 From the remaining backing fabric, cut 5.5 cm (2 in) wide strips to the same length as the two seams that require neatening on the back. The longer piece will probably need lengths to be joined. Fold the strips in half lengthwise, right side out, and sew the long edges together. Centring the seam as you go, press the seam open.

2 Place each strip, seam side down, over each pressed-open seam on the back of the quilt and hand-sew each in place along both edges.

3 Follow the directions for Double binding (see page 128) to fold the strips in half, right sides out, and attach and finish the binding.

4 Make a two-part hanging sleeve from excess backing, if wished (see page 129), then label to finish.

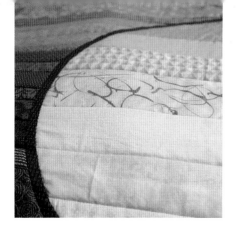

Here, two 'bites' are cut from opposite sides of the quilt and switched places. A strong progression of value from light to dark ensures this effect is clearly visible. The random-width strips are cut in lengths obtainable from fat quarters and joined using an insert of the following fabric in the sequence.

Take a Bite

APPROXIMATE SIZE OF QUILT

150 x 100 cm (59 x 39 in)

SEAM ALLOWANCES

0.75 cm (¼ in) unless otherwise stated

YOU WILL NEED

A fabric width of 110–114 cm (43–44 in) unless otherwise stated. Iron all fabrics before cutting.

- Approximately 32 different fabrics ('fat' quarters or 'fat' eighths) (see page 108) for strip-piecing the quilt top: the smallest possible width for each strip is 4 cm (1½ in)
- 220 cm (86 in) backing fabric
- 50 cm (19½ in) dark print for appliqué semi-circles
- One 'fat' quarter of medium light value for the light half of the binding
- 160 cm (63 in) wadding (batting)
- Sewing thread in neutral shade or to match backing
- Sewing thread in dark to match semi-circle fabric choice
- Template on page 139
- See also Equipment, pages 110–111

CUTTING

❶ From the darkest fabric, cut 3 cm (1⅛ in) wide strips to total 250 cm (100 in) when joined for binding the dark half of the quilt. (A scrap of this fabric is also used for the insert in the final strip at the dark end, see page 84.)

❷ From the backing fabric, cut a length of 160 cm (63 in) for backing and two 56 x 30 cm (22 x 12 in) rectangles for finishing the semi-circles on the quilt back. The remaining fabric will be used later for a hanging sleeve.

❸ From the appliqué semi-circle fabric, cut two 56 x 30 cm (22 x 12 in) rectangles.

❹ From the fabric of medium light value cut strips to the same size as the darkest fabric (above) for binding the light half of the quilt.

MAKING THE STRIPS

1 Arrange the fabrics for the quilt top in the desired value sequence. You can include the fabric chosen for the cut-out bites but avoid using it where the strip sequence would come within these areas. Beginning at the dark end of the sequence, cut strips varying in width between 4 cm (1½ in) and 11.5 cm (4½ in). Decide on the width of the first dark-end strip (not that used for the binding) and cut two strips of that width from the long edge of the fat quarter or eighth. Also from the dark binding fabric, cut a patch of this width by 5.5 cm (2 in) for the insert. Pin the two strips and the insert patch together.

2 Proceed in this way, cutting two strips from each fabric, and varying the widths to suit. Always cut an insert patch from the preceding fabric. Take care to keep the sequence correct by stacking the strips. As you approach the last 50 cm (19½ in) or so, you need to calculate the widths to ensure that all the fabrics can be fitted into the remaining space.

ASSEMBLING THE QUILT

1 Follow the directions for Quilt-as-you-go (see page 125) to layer up the backing and wadding. Thread-baste a straight line at one end for starting work and mark a centre line lengthwise.

2 Work the strip-piecing from the light end: your stack of cut strips should have the lightest set on top. Sew together the first set of strip–insert–strip and press the seams towards the insert.

3 Place this strip on the basted line. Pin and baste the long edges.

4 Piece together the second strip set and press. Place this strip right side down over the first, with long raw edges level and stepping the insert a little to one side of the previous one. Pin and/or baste, then sew.

5 Repeat this process until all the strips are attached. Trim the edges of the quilt, ensuring that the corners are square (**Diagram A**).

6 Make a paper template of a 50 cm (19½ in) diameter semi-circle using the template on page 139. Position this on the long edges of the quilt, once near the dark end and once on the opposite side towards the light end (**Diagram A**). Mark the curve as accurately as possible (or the replacement will not fit well), then cut through all the layers.

A

7 Switch the two cut-outs. Butting the edges together closely, but keeping them flat, sew the join with a wide zigzag stitch (**Diagram B**).

8 On the right side of the semi-circle fabric rectangles, lightly mark out the same 50 cm (19½ in) semi-circle, aligning the flat side with one long edge of the fabric. Measure and mark 1.25 cm (½ in) away from this outline both inside and outside the curve (**Diagram C**).

9 Place one rectangle, right side up, on top of one of the semi-circular cut-outs, exactly matching the drawn centre line of the curve with the butted join. Thread-baste in place. Beginning on the inside curve, and cutting just a short distance at a time, turn in 0.75 cm (¼ in) and sew down by hand as neatly as possible (**Diagram D**). Now cut and sew the outer curve, repeating the process.

10 Finish the reverse of the cut-outs in the same way, using the rectangles of backing fabric.

FINISHING

1 Follow the directions on Binding (see pages 126–128) to join and attach the binding for a 0.75 cm (¼ in) finish. Note that the joins between light and dark will need to be made with particular care at just the right place. Work them both as for a final join but with a straight, not angled, seam.

2 Decide which way you want the quilt to hang: it can be either landscape or portrait format. Make a hanging sleeve and attach accordingly (see page 129), then label the quilt to finish.

Variations

- Use the same appliqué method to add a fabric ring over a circle: cut a circle carefully out of the quilt, rotate it by 90 degrees and butt-join. Then appliqué a ring to conceal the join. Note, however, that the circle must be cut and worked very accurately for this variation to look effective.

- Instead of rotating the circle, as above, cut two or more circles and switch them.

B

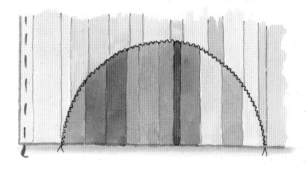

C

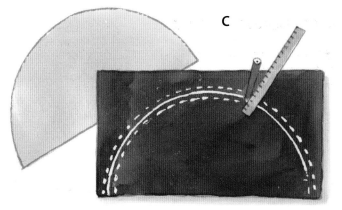

D

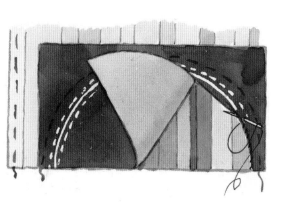

The colour scheme of this quilt is reminiscent of golden evening sunlight striking a snowy scene. The free-embroidered drawings are, perhaps, not for a beginner, but newcomers to quilt-making could replace the drawings with purchased printed panels, framed to bring them to appropriate sizes.

Winter Wonderland

APPROXIMATE SIZE OF QUILT
150 x 150 cm (60 x 60 in)

SEAM ALLOWANCES
0.75 cm (¼ in) unless otherwise stated

YOU WILL NEED
A fabric width of 110–114 cm (43–44 in) unless otherwise stated. Iron all fabrics before cutting.
- 140 cm (54 in) butterscotch 'cracked ice' fabric for border and binding
- Nine to ten 'fat' quarters (see page 108) ranging from off-white, beige, tan and light grey to rust and burnt sugar, including metallics
- Assorted light-coloured, textured fabrics equivalent to 75 cm (29½ in) in seven rectangles of various sizes, for block backgrounds
- 270 cm (108 in) backing fabric
- 160 cm (63 in) low-loft wadding (batting) 160 cm (63 in) wide
- Assorted scraps in same colour range as quarters, minimum 11.5 cm (4½ in) square
- 50 cm (19½ in) tear-away embroidery stabilizer
- Light neutral sewing thread
- Variegated machine-embroidery thread
- Variegated machine-quilting thread
- Templates on page 140
- See also Equipment, pages 110–111

CUTTING

1 From the butterscotch fabric, cut four 125 x 16.5 cm (50 x 6½ in) strips parallel to the selvedge for borders. Also cut 4 cm (1½ in) wide strips to total 625 cm (250 in) binding when joined.

2 Select two fat quarters, one dark and one light, and cut a 9 cm (3½ in) wide strip for the four-patch corner blocks from each.

3 From the light rectangles, cut the following: two 30 x 30 cm (12 x 12 in) squares; one 40 x 20 cm (16 x 8 in) rectangle; two 30 x 20 cm (12 x 8 in) rectangles; one 20 x 20 cm (8 x 8 in) square; and one 20 x 10 cm (8 x 4 in) rectangle for the embroidered blocks. Or vary the mix to suit the fabrics available, noting that measurements need to be in multiples of 10 cm (4 in).

4 For each block, select a coordinating fabric from which to cut 4 cm (1½ in) wide framing strips. They need to be 6.5 cm (2½ in) longer than their respective block size.

5 From the remaining fabrics, including any framing leftovers, cut 11.5 x 11.5 cm (4½ x 4½ in) squares. You need a total of 100.

> ### TIP
> When cutting the 100 squares, start with perhaps two squares of each fabric. Then cut more when you see which fabrics and values are needed.

MAKING THE EMBROIDERED BLOCKS

Following the instructions for Machine-embroidery (see pages 118–119), and any advice printed in your machine manual, practise on some spare fabric before starting the quilt proper. Set up the machine for free-machine embroidery. Note that, here, the desired top thread is wound (by hand if necessary) on to the machine bobbin, because the design is sewn from the back of the work. This allows you to use bold thread that might otherwise shred or break if passing through the machine needle. The resulting image will be easier to see on the finished quilt. Ordinary sewing thread will also work, as long as the tone is dark enough to be visible from a distance, in which case working from the back is not necessary.

❶ Copy the reindeer and tree motifs from page 140 to the desired sizes and reverse them. Trace on to suitably sized pieces of tearaway stabilizer. Centre one, drawn side up, on the wrong side of each block. Baste together, keeping your stitches away from actual drawn lines (**Diagram A**).

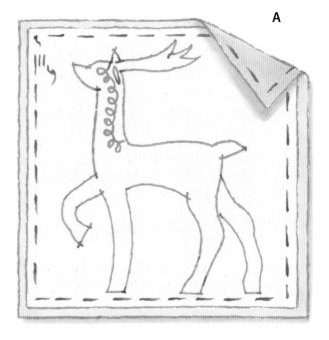

A

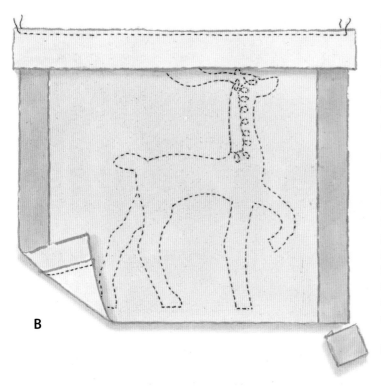

B

❷ Free-embroider the design in a continuous line, as far as possible. For the reindeer, begin at the head by the ear and work around the head, down the front of the body, around the legs, taking a brief detour up towards the tail on the third leg before coming back to the fourth leg, around the tail, along the back and up the neck. Finish by working the eye and the scroll on the neck. The trees are simpler and can be further decorated with extra lines of stitching.

❸ After working the blocks, press.

❹ As free-embroidery can distort or shrink the blocks slightly, true up the blocks now, ensuring the corners are right angles, before sewing on the framing strips. Attach framing strips to opposite sides of the block, press with turnings towards the frame and trim the excess fabric. Now add framing strips to top and bottom (**Diagram B**) and press. Check the block sizes and trim as necessary. They need to be sized in multiples of 10 cm (4 in) plus 1.5 cm (½ in) for seam allowances (So, 31.5 x 31.5 cm/12½ x 12½ in, for example). It is acceptable for framing strips to be of varying widths from block to block.

❺ Remove the stabilizer and press again.

ARRANGING THE BLOCKS

1 Spread the embroidered blocks out, if possible on a design wall.

2 Fill in the space around the blocks with 11.5 x 11.5 cm (4½ x 4½ in) squares, using existing squares to decide which fabrics to repeat. The project here has a darker centre with lighter values towards the border.

3 Cut or make extra patches until you have achieved an area equivalent to 12 squares both vertically and horizontally.

ASSEMBLING THE QUILT

1 Sew the square patches together in groups for attaching to the theme blocks as appropriate. Use a light neutral thread for sewing.

2 Use chain-piecing when possible (see Patchwork techniques, page 115), but take care not to get too far ahead of yourself in order to stick to your design. Press the seams on rows of blocks in opposite directions. Expect to assemble areas such as quarters or two or three sections, vertically or horizontally. These can then be joined. When complete, press the quilt centre carefully.

3 Sew the two strips for making the corner blocks together, pressing the seam towards the darker fabric. Cut eight 9 cm (3½ in) wide slices (**Diagram C**). Sew into four-patch blocks and press.

4 Follow the instructions for Attaching borders (see page 121) to place a border strip to one side of the quilt centre, right sides together, and sew. Press the seam towards the border. Repeat to add the second border to the opposite side.

5 Attach a corner block to each end of the two remaining border strips. Press the seams towards the border fabric. Attach these borders, matching the corner-block seams with the borders already attached.

QUILTING AND FINISHING

1 If copying the design used on this quilt, use the template on page 140 to mark the continuous star motif in the borders, keeping the points clear from the turning that will be taken by the binding.

2 Follow the instructions for Traditional quilting (see pages 122–123) to assemble the quilt layers and baste

3 Machine-quilt the centre, going around the blocks 'in the ditch' (see Machine quilting, page 123), then diagonally through the squares in continuous lines and in the borders. Here, the motifs were outline-quilted by hand for emphasis.

4 Follow the instructions for Binding (see pages 126–128) to finish the quilt. Add a hanging sleeve, if wished (see page 129) and label.

Variation

- Replace the free-machine drawings with hand-embroidered motifs: either panels saved from old household linens or pieces worked specifically for the project.

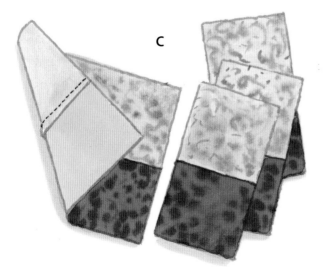

C

This versatile quilt can be used for a child's bed or play mat, or it could hang in a doorway for use as a puppet theatre. Have fun searching for suitable fabrics to use as tree trunks, water, foliage of various colours, earth and sky; different weights and textures can be combined as long as all are washable.

Enchanted Forest

APPROXIMATE SIZE OF QUILT

122 x 90 cm (48 x 36 in)

SEAM ALLOWANCES

0.75 cm (¼ in) unless otherwise stated

YOU WILL NEED

A fabric width of 110–114 cm (43–44 in) unless otherwise stated. Iron all fabrics before cutting.

- 190 cm (72 in) seasonal print backing fabric
- 'Long' or 'fat' quarters (see page 108) of assorted landscape prints: autumn leaves, pebbles, grass, tree bark, plus plains if necessary
- Silk flowers or leaves (**not** plastic)
- Scraps of theme-related fabrics: ladybird print, bugs, ants, etc.
- 125 cm (49½ in) low-loft wadding (batting) plus a few extra scraps
- Neutral sewing thread
- Variegated machine-embroidery thread
- Temporary spray adhesive
- 92 cm (36½ in) bamboo cane for hanging pole
- Sew-on hook and loop fabric fasteners
- Soft toys or puppets
- Tissue paper (optional)
- Ribbon, tape or cord for bag drawstring (optional)
- See also Equipment, pages 110–111

CUTTING

❶ Cut a rectangle of low-loft wadding 122 x 90 cm (48 x 36 in) or to your preferred size.

❷ Cut all remaining fabrics as required.

> **TIP**
> While working, check regularly for fibres clogging the bobbin case and foot. Putting tissue paper between the wadding and the machine can reduce this problem, and it is easily torn away after stitching.

CREATING THE SCENE

1 Play with your fabrics before cutting, trying out positions directly on to the rectangle of wadding until you are satisfied with the colour balance and 'depth' created. Use my quilt as a starting point, but vary the scene as you like. Be sure to include different 'habitats' for your animals, such as earth or grassy bank, trees or bushes, and ensure the areas are large enough to make holes in for the animals. The fabric flap covering the back of each hole should match that on the front of the quilt for that area, so make sure you keep enough fabric back for this.

2 Cut out the trees first, without seam allowances, and lay them directly on the wadding. Cut out and place surrounding fabrics for foliage and ground, allowing at least 2.5 cm (1 in) to tuck under the tree edges where the fabric does not extend to the edges of the wadding (**Diagram A**).

3 Pin more fabrics in place, tucking in extra wadding scraps beneath fabrics that need more relief: remember that you want texture, not a smooth, flat surface. View the quilt from a distance and be prepared to change or rearrange areas.

4 When you are satisfied, follow the instructions for Free-machining (see page 119) and set up your machine with feed dogs down and free-embroidery foot attached, if available, to satin-stitch appliqué all the fabric edges directly on to the wadding. Use appropriate-coloured sewing or machine-embroidery threads.

A

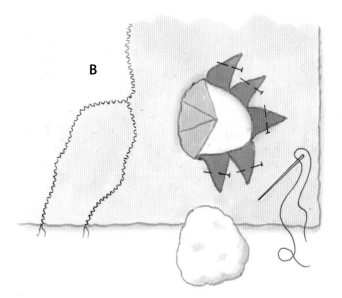

B

COMPLETING THE CONSTRUCTION

1 Cut holes about 8 cm (3 in) in diameter into the top fabrics in the chosen places. The holes do not have to be perfect circles. Cut away slightly larger holes from the wadding behind the fabric holes. Snip into the fabric so that it can be folded in, over the wadding edge, around the hole. Pin and/or thread-baste in place (**Diagram B**). Check that each hole accommodates the relevant animal.

2 Check the quilt size and cut a rectangle of backing fabric that is 2.5 cm (1 in) larger all around. Turn the work over to have the wadding side uppermost. Following the manufacturer's instructions, spray the wadding lightly with fabric glue, avoiding the holes. Centre the backing fabric, right side up, over the sprayed wadding and smooth together. Turn the quilt over again.

3 Pin the layers together around the holes and, working from the front, cut away a small circle in the centre of each hole, through the backing fabric. Turn the quilt over again. Now working from the back, snip into the cut fabric and turn the raw edges into the quilt 'sandwich' so they will not be seen from the front. Pin or baste, then sew around the holes.

4 With the quilt on a flat surface, follow the instructions for Edge-to-edge finishing (see page 129) to work along the sides, folding in the edges of the top and the backing to enclose the wadding. Note that the backing should be turned a little further in than the turned edge of the front, instead of actually edge-to-edge. Pin, then thread-baste.

QUILTING AND FINISHING

1 Following the instructions on Machine-quilting (see page 123) and starting at one edge of the quilt, machine-quilt the different parts of the woodland in appropriate-coloured threads. Change to the Free-machine embroidery method (see page 119) for adding bark details to trees or other details elsewhere on the printed fabrics.

2 Quilt areas of fabric that are plain, mottled or multi-hued with leaf patterns, if desired.

3 Most of the quilt is now stable with machining. Lay it out to see whether you want to add more detail: another toadstool, a fish? Check that the edges of the holes are secure and over-sew them for extra strength if needed. Also, straight-stitch all around the quilt edges.

4 Lay the quilt out and start placing the silk leaves and flowers. These details should look natural, so consider using the reverse of any that seem too bright. On the quilt here, tiny leaves 'float' in the pool, making it seem farther away, while large leaves seem to blow towards us from the large tree on the left. Play until you are happy with the arrangement.

5 Pin in place and view from a distance. When satisfied, machine into place using straight stitch down the centre veins of the leaves, leaving the edges loose. You can sew through overlapping leaves if you wish. Flowers may need bar-tacks rather than complete lines of stitching.

6 Cut out and hem squares of matching fabrics to make the flaps behind each hole. Ensure the hole is completely covered when the flap is in place. Add a hook and loop patch to the base of the square.

7 Pin the squares in place, then hand-stitch the top of the flap to the back of the quilt. Add the corresponding hook and loop patch below the hole to complete the fixing.

8 From the remaining backing fabric, cut and make a hanging sleeve and add a label (see page 129). There ought also to be enough backing fabric remaining to make a simple drawstring bag to hold the toys.

Variations

- Make the quilt to reflect any season by changing the fabrics used.
- Use the same method of construction to make any other scene that would allow imaginative play with a different set of toys, or puppets or dolls. For example, a house with several floors where the holes are windows.

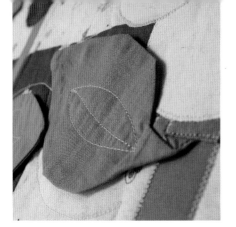

This bright, cheerful quilt will suit both boys and girls. Highly stylized petals, leaves and some butterfly wings made with three-dimensional techniques are ideal for enlivening the surface. This example also includes a few purchased iron-on embroidered motifs.

Spencer's Sunflowers

APPROXIMATE SIZE OF QUILT

123 x 102 cm (48½ x 40 in)

SEAM ALLOWANCES

0.75 cm (¼ in) unless otherwise stated

YOU WILL NEED

A fabric width of 110–114 cm (43–44 in) unless otherwise stated. Iron all fabrics before cutting.

- 115 cm (45 in) 'sky' print for the background
- One 'fat' quarter (see page 108) solid blue for strip-piecing the background and binding
- One 'fat' quarter blue ground floral print for strip-piecing the background
- 50 cm (19½ in) solid green for leaves, stems and binding
- 50 cm (19½ in) red (solid or mottled) for butterfly wings and binding
- 60 cm (22½ in) solid yellow for petals, bee bodies and binding
- One 'fat' quarter bee-print or alternative yellow for petals
- One 'fat' quarter black/yellow print for bee bodies and flower centres

- Scraps of beige for butterfly bodies
- One 'fat' quarter white for bee wings
- 150 cm (60 in) backing
- 130 cm (51 in) wadding (batting)
- 120 cm (45 in) fusible webbing
- Yellow, green and neutral sewing thread
- Machine-embroidery or sewing thread in red, yellow, white, beige and green
- Iron-on (fusible) embroidered motifs, optional
- Templates on page 141
- See also Equipment, pages 110–111

CUTTING

❶ From the 'sky' print, cut five 21.5 cm (8½ in) wide strips the length of the fabric.

❷ From the two strip-piecing fabrics, cut 21.5 cm (8½ in) wide strips of varying length, between 6.5 cm (2½ in) and 21.5 cm (8½ in). This example uses five strips of floral print and eight of solid blue.

❸ From the green fabric, and parallel to the selvedge, cut nine 20 x 17.5 cm (8 x 7 in) rectangles for the leaves and a 50 x 31 cm (18 x 12 in) rectangle for the stems.

❹ From the yellow fabric, cut six 31 x 23 cm (12 x 9 in) rectangles. (Bee bodies and strips for binding will be cut later.) Also, cut two rectangles of the same size from the bee-print fabric.

❺ Cut the remaining fabrics as needed.

MAKING THE BACKGROUND STRIPS

① Use neutral sewing thread to strip-piece the patches of blue floral and solid blue into and/or at one end of the sky strips. Seams need not line up when they are sewn together later. Every strip needs at least one extra patch to bring it to the required length of 123.5 cm (48½ in). Press seams towards the darker fabrics.

② Do not sew the strips together yet, as it is easier to appliqué them separately. Lay them out and decide their order, then label accordingly from left to right.

WORKING THE APPLIQUÉ

① Begin by making the three-dimensional shapes. Fold a leaf rectangle in half, right sides together, to 10 x 17.5 cm (4 x 7 in). Draw the leaf shape on one side, using the template on page 141. Sew around the shape on the marked line, using green thread. Cut out, leaving a 0.75 cm (¼ in) turning and clipping into the curves (**Diagram A**). Turn right side out and press. Repeat to make nine leaves.

② Cut two 20 x 23 cm (8 x 9 in) red rectangles for butterfly wings and fold each in half, right sides together, to 20 x 11.5 cm (8 x 4½ in). Repeat the process to make two three-dimensional butterfly wings (template on page 141). When cutting out, leave 0.5 cm (scant ¼ in) seam allowance on the straight body edge. Baste this edge closed. If wished, machine-quilt in red thread 0.5 cm (scant ¼ in) from the curved edge.

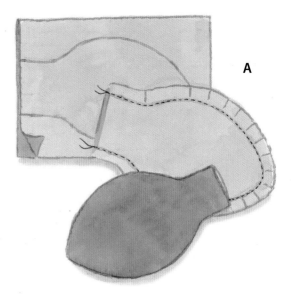

A

③ Fold a yellow rectangle in half to 31 x 11.5 cm (12 x 4½ in), and mark out petal shapes as shown in **Diagram B**, leaving 1.5 cm (½ in) space between them. Sew on the drawn lines, stitching from one to the next without cutting the thread. Cut out and turn as directed for the leaves. (Use a chopstick or knitting needle to help turn the petals out, but do not worry if some are not exact.) Repeat on the remaining five yellow rectangles and the two bee-print rectangles. You should get eight petals per rectangle, making 48 yellow and 16 bee-print for a total of 64. You need 60 for five flowers with 12 petals each.

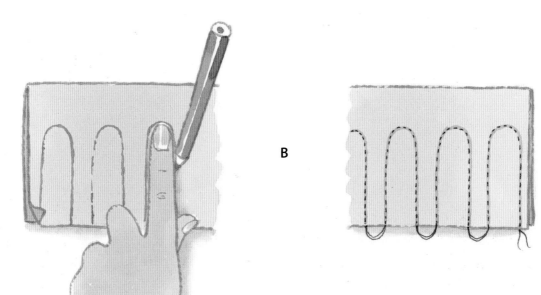

B

4 Follow the directions for Appliqué techniques (see pages 116–117) to cut a rectangle of fusible webbing to 50 x 31 cm (18 x 12 in) and fuse to the wrong side of the remaining green rectangle. When they are cool, cut into 50 x 2 cm (18 x ¾ in) strips for stems, noting that they should not all be the same length. Centre a stem on each sky strip. Where you want a leaf, there must be a join in the stem. Do not fuse the stems to the background yet.

5 From the black/yellow print, using the flower-centre circle template, trace off, fuse and cut out five centres.

6 Repeat the steps for fusible appliqué to prepare five butterfly bodies, five white bee wings, and eight red butterfly wings. To make a bee body, trace and fuse the main shape on to yellow fabric, then fuse on stripes of black/yellow print before cutting out the body. Make four more bee bodies.

ATTACHING THE APPLIQUÉ

1 Arrange the elements on each strip, positioning them to match the illustration or as you prefer. Note that each strip has a butterfly and a bee as well as a sunflower and that some stems have two leaves.

2 To attach the appliqué, begin by removing the backing paper from the stems. Fuse the top section of each stem, then, following the advice for stitching, zigzag- or satin-stitch the long edges with green machine-embroidery thread. Position a leaf, angled upwards, and baste in place before fusing the next stem section. Zigzag-stitch the edges, including across the end of the stem where the leaf is inserted. Continue until all the stems and leaves are fixed.

3 Fuse the bee wings and then their bodies. Zigzag the wings in white, then the bodies in yellow, including the body stripes. In the same way, add three flat butterflies and finish with matching red and beige zigzagging.

4 Now fuse the flower centre circles over the top of the stems. Position 12 petals per flower around a centre, having the raw edges facing outwards from the centre, and baste (**Diagram C**). You may find an elastic band useful to keep the petals together in the middle while you sew. Sew around the petals to attach. Then remove the band, allowing the petals to fall outwards. Arrange neatly into a circle, pin or baste, then sew round again 1 cm (scant ½ in) from the fold and hiding the raw edges below (**Diagram D**). This method encourages the petals to stand away from the background, as shown in the photograph on page 98.

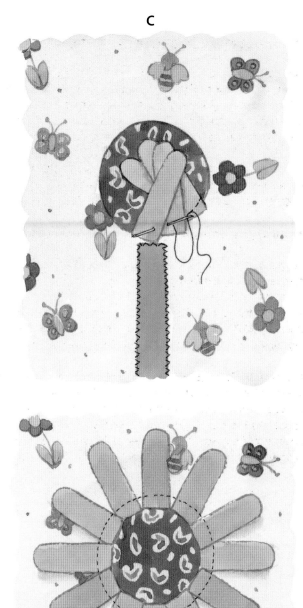

C

D

5 For the three-dimensional butterflies, first fuse one red wing to the background and stitch the curved edges. Now place a three-dimensional wing with the basted edge overlapping the straight fused wing by 0.5 cm (scant ¼ in). Pin or baste 1 cm (½ in) away from the edge. Now fuse the body so that it covers the edge of the wing and zigzag-stitch to finish.

ASSEMBLING THE QUILT TOP

1 Join the pieced strips together, using neutral thread on the machine and pressing the vertical seams away from the centre. Take care to avoid catching the free petals and leaves in these seams.

2 Fold the leaves downwards and sideways into interesting positions. Using green machine-embroidery thread, sew each leaf in place, using a stylized leaf motif centred on each one. It is more interesting if these are worked freely rather than using a template (see detail photograph on page 94).

3 If using the optional purchased embellishments, fuse them on to the quilt now.

QUILTING AND FINISHING

1 Follow the instructions for Traditional quilting (see pages 122–123) to layer up the backing, wadding and top.

2 Follow the instructions for Machine-quilting (see page 123) to work in yellow thread echo-quilting approximately 1 cm (⅜ in) away from the stems, and continuing around the overlapping motifs. For the sunflowers, lift the petals out of the way and quilt a circle about 2.5 cm (1 in) away from where the petals are attached.

3 Follow the instructions for Binding (see pages 126–128) to finish the quilt using strips cut from the solid colours, red, blue, green and yellow, as available. For a neat finish, try to avoid changing colour at a corner.

4 Make a hanging sleeve from the excess backing fabric and label the quilt (see page 129) to finish.

Variations

- Vary the size of project by changing the number of strips, perhaps to fit a specific wall space, or by altering the length of the strips.

- Instead of having the solid blue inserts, piece in strips of white to look like a fence; or instead of the sunflowers growing from the lower edge, let them grow out of plant pots appliquéd in a row.

- Make a tall flower on a single background strip, perhaps cut slightly wider, bound and finished to use as a height record as the children of the family grow up. Stitch on a short strip of ribbon to mark the height and add the name with fabric pen.

This project consists of a background 'quilt sky' to which kites are sewn. The kites themselves are made with three layers and can be filled with wadding left from previous projects. The simple concept of this hanging offers plenty of potential for creating your own unique versions.

Bright Kites

APPROXIMATE SIZE OF QUILT
89 x 107 cm (35 x 42 in)

SEAM ALLOWANCES
0.75 cm (¼ in) unless otherwise stated

YOU WILL NEED
A fabric width of 110–114 cm (43–44 in) unless otherwise stated. Iron all fabrics before cutting.
- 100 cm (39 in) cotton backing fabric
- 150 cm (60 in) sky print for background/binding
- 70 cm (27 in) of one rainbow-colour cotton fabric (turquoise here)
- 50 cm (19½ in) of two rainbow-colour cotton fabrics (yellow and purple here)
- One 'fat' quarter (see page 108) of remaining rainbow colours (red, orange, green and blue)
- Craft-size wadding (batting), 90 x 115 cm (36 x 45 in) or 115 x 115 cm (45 x 45 in) for sky
- Three wadding (batting) rectangles, one each of 55 x 100 cm (21½ x 39 in); 53 x 31 cm (21 x 12 in); 41 x 26 cm (16 x 10 in)
- Sewing thread
- Hand- and machine-embroidery threads for cord-making
- Invisible machine-quilting thread or shaded machine-embroidery thread (optional)
- See also Equipment, pages 110–111

CUTTING

1 From the sky fabric, cut four 3 cm (1⅛ in) wide strips from one long selvedge and set aside for binding.

2 From the turquoise fabric, cut a 55 x 100 cm (21½ x 39 in) rectangle to back the large kite.

3 From the yellow fabric, cut a 53 x 31 cm (21 x 12 in) rectangle to back the middle-size kite.

4 From the purple fabric, cut a 41 x 26 cm (16 x 10 in) rectangle to back the small kite.

5 Follow the plans for the large and medium kites to cut strips from the rainbow fabrics to the required widths and lengths (**Diagrams A and B**). For the small kite, cut rectangles to the sizes shown in **Diagram C**.

6 From leftover scraps of fabric, cut rectangles for the tail bows as follows:
Large kite: 7 x 15 cm (2¾ x 6 in); seven bows suggested
Medium kite: 3.5 x 13 cm (2¼ x 5 in); six bows suggested
Small kite: 5 x 10 cm (2 x 4 in); five bows suggested

A

7.5 x 11.5 cm (3 x 4½ in)

28 x 11.5 cm (11 x 4½ in)

20 x 11.5 cm (8 x 4½ in)

10 x 11.5 cm (4 x 4½ in)

20 x 11.5 cm (8 x 4½ in)

28 x 11.5 cm (11 x 4½ in)

28 x 11.5 cm (11 x 4½ in)

20 x 11.5 cm (8 x 4½ in)

25.5 x 11.5 cm (10 x 4½ in)

48 x 11.5 cm (19 x 4½ in)

25.5 x 11.5 cm (10 x 4½ in)

20 x 11.5 cm (8 x 4½ in)

71 x 11.5 cm (28 x 4½ in)

15 x 11.5 cm (6 x 4½ in)

10 x 11.5 cm (4 x 4½ in)

7.5 x 11.5 cm (3 x 4½ in)

B

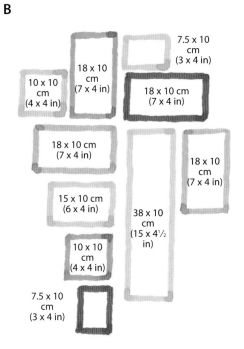

7.5 x 10 cm (3 x 4 in)

10 x 10 cm (4 x 4 in)

18 x 10 cm (7 x 4 in)

18 x 10 cm (7 x 4 in)

18 x 10 cm (7 x 4 in)

18 x 10 cm (7 x 4 in)

15 x 10 cm (6 x 4 in)

38 x 10 cm (15 x 4½ in)

10 x 10 cm (4 x 4 in)

7.5 x 10 cm (3 x 4 in)

C

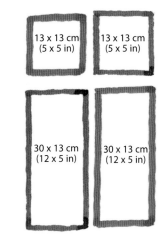

13 x 13 cm (5 x 5 in)

13 x 13 cm (5 x 5 in)

30 x 13 cm (12 x 5 in)

30 x 13 cm (12 x 5 in)

D

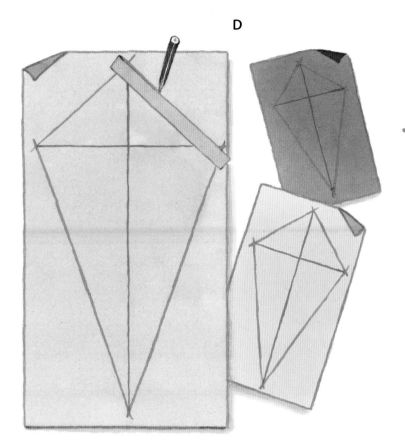

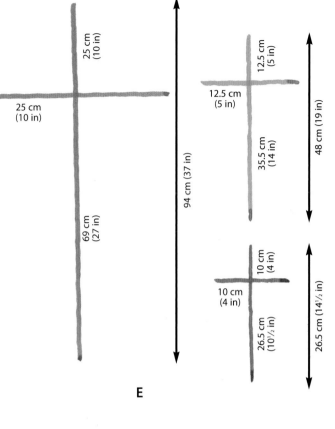

25 cm (10 in)
25 cm (10 in)
94 cm (37 in)
69 cm (27 in)

12.5 cm (5 in)
12.5 cm (5 in)
35.5 cm (14 in)
48 cm (19 in)

10 cm (4 in)
10 cm (4 in)
26.5 cm (10½ in)
26.5 cm (14½ in)

E

MAKING THE BACKGROUND QUILT

❶ Spread the backing fabric, right side down, on a flat surface with the width of the fabric running from top to bottom of the quilt. Over this place the wadding then the sky fabric, right side up, and pin- or thread-baste the layers together.

❷ Follow the instructions on Machine-quilting (see page 123) to stitch across the sky print using either sewing thread that matches the fabric, invisible quilting thread or shaded machine-embroidery thread. Keep the lines simple and even, not more than about 15–20 cm (6–8 in) apart. Alternatively, stitch flowing lines that suggest wind currents.

❸ Trim the quilt edges to the desired size, ensuring the corners are truly square. Follow the instructions on Binding (see pages 126–128) to prepare the quilt edges for binding.

❹ Join the binding strips and attach to the quilt. Hang the completed 'sky' somewhere safe while you make the kites.

MAKING THE KITES

❶ To piece the kites, follow the cutting diagrams in **Diagrams A** and **B** to join the appropriate strips that make up the quarters of the large and medium-size kites. Press the seams open.

❷ Join the four quarters of each kite together. The little kite only needs its four rectangles to be joined (**Diagram C**). Press these seams open also. Put aside.

❸ On the wrong side of the turquoise backing rectangle, draw a vertical centre line and mark off 94 cm (37 in). Measure 25 cm (10 in) down from one end and mark a horizontal line at right angles, extending 25 cm (10 in) on both sides. Draw lines to connect the ends of these lines (**Diagram D**). The resulting outline will be your sewing line.

❹ Repeat the process to mark up the yellow and purple rectangles for the medium and small kites, using the lengths in **Diagram E**.

5 Starting with the little kite, layer together the small wadding rectangle, the pieced kite front, right side up and the backing rectangle, wrong side up. Insert a pin at the centre of the backing fabric, where the lines cross and on into the centre of the pieced kite front. In the same way locate the remaining four points of your drawing on the backing with the corresponding seams on the pieced kite front. Pin thoroughly between.

6 Matching thread to kite backing and keeping to the drawn outline, sew around the kite shape, turning the corners accurately, leaving an opening on one long side for turning right sides out. Secure the threads at the ends of your stitching.

7 Trim all the layers to leave a 0.75 cm (¼ in) seam allowance beyond the stitching line. Carefully trim away the wadding from the allowance.

8 Turn the kite right side out. Use a knitting needle or similar to get the corners and point as sharp as possible. Press to achieve edges as crisp as possible, then sew the opening closed by hand.

9 Repeat the process to make the medium then the large kite.

MAKING CORDS FOR THE KITE TAILS

1 Make a practice cord of about 30 cm (12 in) first. Cut several strands of any hand-embroidery threads that you may have. Knot together near one end. These strands form the core of your cord.

2 Set the machine for medium-width zigzag stitch. Place the core centrally under the sewing machine foot, grasping the knot and the machine thread tails behind the presser foot.

3 Start sewing and pull steadily on the core to draw it through the machine as you sew. The zigzag stitch should swing from one side of the core to the other, binding the threads closely together. Adjust the width and stitch length as required.

4 Do not worry if you have sewn to one side of the core in places. When you reach the end, cut the cord free from the machine then simply load it in and sew it again. Two passes through the machine should be sufficient, but if you are not satisfied with the look or size of it, you can run it through again, perhaps with a different colour thread or having added a few more lengths of thread to increase the volume.

5 For the kite tails (long enough for tying on the bows), the threads for the core should be cut as follows:

Large kite: 76 cm (30 in) long; seven strands suggested
Medium kite: 66 cm (26 in) long; five/six strands suggested
Small kite: 56 cm (22 in) long; four strands suggested

6 If colours are limited for core threads, add more interest by machine-sewing in colours not present in the core or using different colours in the needle and bobbin.

ASSEMBLING THE WALL HANGING

1 Pin the kites to the right side of the sky quilt either following the illustration or varying the position to please yourself. Leave space towards the lower edge for the tails. As the kites are complete fabric objects, they may project a little beyond the quilt edges, as here.

2 When satisfied with the arrangement, pin the kites at right angles along the centre lines. As you go, tuck the end of the correct kite tail cord under the lower point of each kite. With matching cotton or invisible monofilament thread, stitch carefully through all the layers across each kite in both directions. If the kite projects beyond the edge of the quilt, sew up to, but not across, the binding. Secure the ends neatly.

3 Working on the ironing board, press the long edges of each rectangle for the tail bows to meet in the middle. Then fold the short ends towards the centre to overlap by about 2.5 cm (1 in), and press.

4 Tie the bows on to the cords, spacing them evenly. Using thread to match the sky fabric, make two to three stitches at each bow, securing it to the sky with the tail in a curve that you like.

5 Make a hanging sleeve and label (see page 129) to finish.

Variations

- Simplify the kites by making the large and medium versions like the small one, using just two colours.
- Instead of three different sizes of kite, use just the little version but make perhaps five in assorted colour combinations, which would suit working with scraps rather than buying lots of colours.

Materials, Equipment & Techniques

Just as an investment in good materials and tools is repaid in the quality of the finished article, so too is the investment of time spent learning good technique. Satsifying quilt-making can be achieved with simple basic techniques. However, a number of projects offer the newcomer an opportunity to build on those skills, acquiring new ones that will increase future options.

Materials

Quilting materials are widely available from department stores, fabric shops and specialist craft shops, by mail order and on the Internet. If your work is to look good, be durable and comfortable to use, it is important that you use the most appropriate materials for each project.

FABRIC

For the best results, use similar weight fabric for an entire project. Most projects in this book use 100 per cent cotton, which is easy to work with and presses well. Cotton flannel also behaves well but the thickness of the fabric makes it less suitable for fine detail.

A few projects require more unusual fabrics to add varied textures and finishes to the quilts. These may not be available in quilting shops but can be found in bridal departments or shops selling dance-wear fabrics.

Newcomers to quilt-making often have to start from scratch by buying all the fabrics for one project before beginning. However, any pieces left over will form the basis of a 'stash' to which you can add fabrics that catch your eye, whether you have an immediate use for them or not. Gradually this means that when a project requires 'scraps' of a colour, you will not have to buy every time.

'Fat' quarters refers to a method of cutting a metre (yard) of fabric into quarters by halving it one way then the other to produce square-like shapes, rather than cutting it into four strips, or 'long' quarters. A 'fat' eighth is simply half a 'fat' quarter.

WADDING (BATTING)

This is the soft filling that goes inside a quilt. It is generally described by weight; for the projects in this book, you are advised to use nothing heavier than 50 g (2 oz). Wadding types described as needle-punched, compressed or low-loft – according to the method of construction – look flatter than the standard type but are, in fact, the same weight and just as warm. They suit machine-quilting because they are less 'bouncy'.

Most wadding is white, or natural, although dark (charcoal) products also exist for use inside dark-coloured quilts. Should any fibres from the wadding work through to the outside of the quilt – a process known as 'bearding' – they will not show in the way that light wadding would.

Wadding can be made of different fibres. Polyester is the most common and economical, but cotton is also widely available, as is wool. Both cotton and wool wadding are generally produced with a percentage of polyester to stabilize them, allowing the quilting lines to be further apart. Cotton is popular for machine-quilting but can be hard to hand-quilt. Wool, although rather more expensive, is fine, wonderfully warm and easy to hand- or machine-quilt – but would be wasted on quilts made for wall hangings.

Whatever product you buy, you should read and follow carefully the manufacturer's instructions for preparing the wadding, if necessary, and during its life. Cotton wadding can shrink, so you may be advised to pre-wash it before putting it into your quilt. Polyester needs no preparation so is good for eager beginners.

Wadding can be bought either in pre-cut packages of popular sizes or from the roll. Time spent learning about the various products available will be repaid both by good end results and the knowledge that you are buying wisely.

THREAD

Most piecing is worked with cotton machine-sewing thread, which is widely available in an extensive range of colours to match most fabrics. It can also be used for appliqué and machine-quilting. With scrap projects it is often impossible to match thread to both in a pair of patches, so neutral grey or beige thread may be the answer. When sewing pairs that are light and dark, choose light thread: any stray tails of dark thread may show through a lighter fabric.

'Invisible' thread, which comes in clear or smoke, is suggested for some of the projects. It is a monofilament nylon thread that is ideal for machine-quilting, used for the top thread through the needle with regular sewing thread in the bobbin. It may also be used for sewing on beads – but take care to secure the ends well, as they may uncoil by themselves later. This thread can melt if subjected to a hot iron but this is not usually an issue, as hot irons are not good for wadding either.

The majority of projects in this book are machine-quilted for speed, but if you have the time and inclination you might wish to quilt by hand. Hand-quilting thread is strong, often waxed to slide through the layers without shredding, and is available in a wide variety of colours.

Machine-embroidery threads are needed for a number of projects. They may be made of various fibres, such as rayon, and may include metallic as well as shaded and variegated products. They can be worked with regular thread in the bobbin below, but if you expect to use them often it is worth buying plain machine-embroidery thread in basic colours such as white and brown to load on to the bobbin. As this thread is finer than regular sewing cotton, more of it can be wound on to the bobbin, which means that you can sew for longer before refilling.

Always check the tension and stitch appearance when changing either thread or stitch pattern, as these are very sensitive to tension control. Generally, lower tensions are needed for embroidery to avoid drawing the bobbin thread to the front of the work or tightening the base fabric into puckers.

Although basting (tacking) thread is available, many quilters use up ends of spools or unwanted colours left on bobbins for basting. While some contrast of colour helps when removing, avoid using bright or dark threads as they may leave traces of colour on light fabrics.

INTERFACING

A wide variety of woven and non-woven interfacings are available, but only limited types are required for the projects in this book. The lightest weight of iron-on non-woven interfacing can be used to stabilize special fabrics, such as those used for Coffee and Cream (see pages 78–81). Anything very lightweight, slippery or prone to fraying can be tamed in this way. It makes a small difference to the feel of the fabric but in hangings this is not a problem. Heavier weight interfacing is needed for Christmas Baubles (see pages 48–53).

FUSIBLE WEBBING

Basically, this is a web of heat-sensitive 'glue', most often attached to backing paper upon which motifs can be drawn, and is used for attaching cut-out fabric shapes to a background fabric. 'No-sew' types are available, so you must be sure to buy fusible webbing specifically for sewing. Once in place, the shapes do not fray. Nevertheless, in quilting they are usually enhanced with an outline of zigzag or satin stitch in matching or contrasting colour thread (see Appliqué techniques: Finishing, page 117). Always follow the manufacturer's instructions to obtain the best results. It is usually cheaper to buy fusible webbing off the roll when you need it rather than in small packs of ready-cut pieces. Always keep it as flat as possible, neither tightly rolled nor folded, and avoid damp.

Equipment

Quilting can be enjoyed with the minimum of equipment, and if you sew already, you probably have most of the tools you'll need. Various specialist items are popular with quilters because they speed up work and improve accuracy. As your interest in quilt-making grows, it is worth looking for quilting shops and fairs to stay informed about the latest products.

BASIC KIT

There are a number of tools that are standard in a quilter's basic equipment:
- Paper- and fabric-cutting scissors
- Fine-pointed small scissors
- Unpicker
- Small safety pins
- Pins and pin cushion (glass-headed pins are easier to find and remove)
- Thimble
- Quilter's 300 cm (120 in) tape measure
- Metre rule or yardstick
- Iron and ironing board

Needles for hand-sewing
- Sharps, for general handwork
- Betweens, for quilting
- Straws, long needles, for speed-basting

Needles for machine-sewing
- Universal size 80, for piecing and quilting
- Universal 70, for delicate fabrics
- Embroidery, for embroidery threads

Sewing machine
A straight-stitch sewing machine can be used but a swing-needle machine that does zigzag stitching is necessary for a number of appliqué projects. Such machines often also feature embroidery stitches, which you can experiment with for more decorative results (see Machine-embroidery techniques, pages 118–119).

Rotary cutting set

Consisting of a rotary cutter, a self-healing cutting mat and assorted thick, printed, plastic rulers, this combination of tools has revolutionized the world of quilting and patchwork. It speeds up the process of cutting by eliminating the need for making and marking round templates and by allowing multiple layers of fabric to be cut with a single pass of the blade.

A cutter resembles a pizza wheel with removable blades and a safety guard. The blade is exceptionally sharp and you must engage the guard when laying down the tool after every cut. Several makers produce different sizes and styles of cutter, including designs to assist people with grip problems. The cutter must always be used on a self-healing cutting mat to avoid damaging the blade. Again, different sizes are available, but a mat measuring 42 x 59.5 cm (16½ x 23½ in or A2) is a useful size for beginners.

The plastic rulers come printed with metric or imperial measurements, for example 45 x 10 cm or 12 x 6 in. The printed grid includes 0.25 cm, 0.5 cm and 0.75 cm divisions on metric rulers and ¼ in divisions on imperial rulers. The thickness of the ruler allows the cutter to follow its edge safely. The most accurate results come from keeping to the same maker for all your rulers. (See also Rotary cutting techniques, pages 112–113).

Marking supplies

An HB pencil is basic and cheap and suits many marking needs – for example, tracing appliqué motifs and marking quilting designs. A silver pencil is also versatile, marking both light and dark fabrics, and therefore suitable for mixed printed fabrics. A pencil crayon of a deeper shade than the fabric can be useful for marking quilting lines.

Tailor's chalk is available either as a pencil or in a 'chakoner', which holds chalk powder and delivers it on to the fabric in a fine line. Chalk or light-coloured pencil crayons are useful for marking dark fabrics.

Erasable fabric markers can be useful for transferring designs on to fabrics. Two types exist: vanishing and water-soluble. Take care not to iron over either type, however, as this will make them permanent. Exposure to full sunlight has the same effect. Vanishing markers simply fade away after a short time, and are therefore suitable only for marking the immediate next step of a project. Water-soluble markers must be washed away once that step is complete.

Masking tape

This is very popular with quilters for marking straight quilting lines. Different widths exist to suit varying needs – for example 0.75 cm (¼ in) masking tape can be placed next to a seam for outline or echo quilting. Only apply tape to the length you expect to sew immediately. Do not leave tape on the quilt surface, especially not in the sun,

because it may leave a sticky residue. Lengths of tape can be used several times before replacing, which makes this process cost effective.

OPTIONAL EXTRAS

In addition to the basic kit there are other pieces of equipment that can make life easier and speed up some of the quilt-making processes.

Temporary spray adhesive

This is an aerosol glue for holding the quilt layers together without pinning or thread-basting. You spray it on to the wrong side of the backing fabric and then spread the wadding carefully over the top. You then spray the wadding and place the quilt top, right side up, on top of that. The product allows for re-positioning. The adhesion diminishes over time and washes out later. Always use in a well-ventilated space, following instructions for use closely. Do not substitute products sold for mounting artwork or photographs, as these are highly flammable.

Squared paper

This is useful for planning variations of designs, drawing designs up to scale and working out how best to cut fabric. Buy either metric or imperial to suit your working preference.

Hoops

Plastic and metal or wooden hoops may be used to tension fabric when machine-embroidering. Some machines fail to perform well without having taut fabric, especially for tasks such as free-machining (see Winter Wonderland, pages 86–89). Larger wooden hoops are popular when hand-quilting.

Light box

If you intend to do much sewing, a light box would be a very useful acquisition. It is ideal for tracing through light-coloured fabric for embroidery and for reversing a design for appliqué by tracing over the back of a photocopy. You can buy small light boxes quite cheaply. Taping your work to a sunny window works almost as well but is not quite so comfortable to work at.

Rotary Cutting

The combination of cutter, mat and chunky plastic rulers has reduced the need for templates when cutting out for many patchwork projects. It is quick and, when used carefully, accurate. However, one can just as quickly cut a pile of patches to the wrong size, so it is worth practising with some spare fabric. The instructions below are for right-handed users. Left-handed users should reverse them.

PREPARING YOUR FABRIC

1 Start with a single layer of ironed fabric that almost fits the mat. Find one side that is true to the grain, such as the selvedge, and align it with one of the printed gridlines on the mat. Fabric is usually cut right side up.

2 To trim away the selvedge, first place the ruler with its right-hand edge parallel to, and 0.75 cm (¼ in) away from, the selvedge. Also have a crosswise line on the ruler in line with a crosswise line on the mat.

3 Hold the ruler with the left hand. Positioning the ring finger against the left edge of the ruler can help to keep it in place (**Diagram A**).

4 Take the cutter in the right hand, flat side towards the ruler and the screw away from it, and disengage the guard.

5 Always cut away from you. Position the cutter to the right of the ruler, almost touching the bare mat just before the fabric, in order to cut right from the very edge. Bring the side of the blade towards the thickness of the ruler and, when it touches, put the blade on to the mat. This avoids damage to both the blade and the ruler.

6 Hold the cutter at about 45 degrees to the mat and roll it away from you across the bare bit of mat, continuing over the fabric to the bare mat beyond. Steady, downward pressure is needed to avoid uncut sections, which are a nuisance.

7 When you have cut across the fabric, stop and immediately close the guard before laying the cutter down. Without disturbing the main fabric, slide the ruler away to the left and remove the trimmings.

8 Now straighten one end of the fabric at a right angle to the trimmed selvedge. Place the ruler across the fabric, right-hand edge near the edge to be trimmed. Align a crossline on the ruler with the trimmed selvedge. As above, cut away from you across the fabric.

9 Always prepare fabric in this way to ensure a truly square corner before cutting patches. Avoid disturbing the prepared cloth by turning the cutting mat around so that the straightened side is on the left-hand side ready for cutting.

A

CUTTING STRIPS

❶ Cut strips of the required width from the prepared, now left-hand, side of the cloth, calculating the sizes to include seam allowances. For example, a strip with a finished width of 5 cm (2 in) must be cut 6.5 cm (2½ in) wide to include a 0.75 cm (¼ in) seam allowance on both sides. Place the ruler along the entire length of the fabric, so that the correct printed line matches up with the prepared edge of the fabric.

❷ Follow steps 3 to 7 above to cut the right number of fabric strips.

❸ To cut widths greater than those printed on the ruler, use the measurements printed on the cutting mat instead.

CUTTING SQUARES AND RECTANGLES

❶ To cut squares, align a strip lengthwise with a gridline on the mat. Place the ruler the required distance over the left end of the strip, checking that this line is at right angles to the long edges of the strip before cutting off the first square. Repeat until no more complete squares can be cut from the strip.

❷ To cut rectangles, work in exactly the same way as for cutting squares, first choosing which measurement to cut for the first strips. For example, rectangles to finish 7.5 x 10 cm (3 x 4 in) need to be cut 9 x 11.5 cm (3½ x 4½ in). This means strips can be cut either 9 cm (3½ in) wide and then divided up at 11.5 cm (4½ in) intervals, or vice versa.

❸ Stack cut patches tidily. If not sewing them immediately, store them flat in a labelled envelope or ziplock bag.

CUTTING HALF-SQUARE TRIANGLES

❶ You make this widely used shape first by cutting squares and then dividing them once diagonally. Each square produces two triangles, so for ten triangles you need cut only five squares.

❷ To calculate the size of square to cut, start with the required finished size and add 2.25 cm (⅞ in) for all seam allowances. For example, if the required triangle is half of a 10 cm (4 in) square, adding 2.25 cm (⅞ in) means cutting squares measuring 12.25 x 12.25 cm (4⅞ x 4⅞ in), as described above.

❸ Place each square on the mat, with two opposite corners aligned on a gridline. Line the ruler up with the same gridline and cut away from you to divide the square into two right-angled triangles.

TIP
Even with practice, the cut edge may 'drift' off at a slight angle when cutting many patches, so true up the end frequently.

CUTTING MORE LAYERS

When you feel more confident, try cutting more than one layer of fabric at a time, starting with just two fabrics. Iron each to remove creases, then iron the two together, both right side up so that they cling together. More layers need greater downward pressure on the blade. Uneven pressure may result in lower layers of cloth not being fully cut. As you succeed, progress to more layers – a small cutter with a sharp blade can cut up to six layers and a large cutter up to ten.

Sometimes the extra layers are the result of wanting to cut a larger piece of fabric that does not fit on the mat. This means folding the fabric to fit. Generally, a single fold is best placed close to you so that, as you cut away from you, the blade rolls towards the free ends of the cloth. If the fabric is too wide to be folded once only, fold it in a concertina manner. Take care that the folds are parallel to the straight edges of the cloth and that cutting will be at right angles to the edges and the folds. Otherwise, the cut strips will not be straight.

Care and maintenance

- Establish good working habits: never lay down the cutter without engaging the safety guard first.

- Never leave the cutting mat leaning against anything warm, such as a radiator, or in sunlight, as it will warp.

- Clear the mat of unwanted objects such as pins before cutting, as running over a pin will damage the blade.

- Avoid catching the blade on the edge or corner of the plastic ruler, which will damage both blade and ruler. Practise presenting the cutter towards the thickness of the ruler from the side, just above the surface of the mat, rather than with a chopping action from above.

- Never lay the mat over something precious, such as another quilt.

Patchwork

The joining together of fabric shapes is known as 'piecing' and the resulting fabric is called 'patchwork'. The projects in this book are designed to be relatively quick to work, so it is assumed that a machine will be used for piecing.

Even with the simplest of projects, accuracy is important if the end product is to finish up the intended size. Therefore begin by checking that you can sew an accurate 0.75 cm (¼ in) seam allowance. An inspection of both metric and imperial rulers will show that the metric seam allowance is not an actual conversion of the imperial one. **This means that, when working, you must keep to the same measuring system throughout any given project.**

SEWING AN ACCURATE SEAM ALLOWANCE

There are three ways to sew an accurate seam allowance.

Check the presser foot

To use imperial measurements, first study your machine and its manual. You may find that the machine has a presser foot designed in such a way that, when the needle is in the central sewing position and the fabric is placed with the raw edge in line with the right-hand edge of the foot, it will sew an exact ¼ in seam. It may be called a "¼ in' foot or, perhaps, a 'patchwork' foot. If you have one of these, simply take two of your practice patches, sew, press and check that the results match the ¼ in achieved when cutting. You can also use the method below (Make your own guide) to check other feet of the machine. If the edge of the foot aligns with the edge of the ruler, then it is probably usable as a guide.

Check the throat plate

Sewing machines have a throat plate, pierced to allow the needle through, and on to which the presser foot is lowered. This may be marked with lines for the most widely used seam allowances. Check whether these are metric or imperial, which will determine the measuring system you should use. Sew two patches together using the throat plate marking as a guide. Press and check for accuracy.

Make your own guide

If neither of the above options is available, make your own guide:

❶ Decide on metric or imperial measurements. Have a plastic cutting ruler of the chosen system, some narrow masking tape and a craft knife.

❷ Slide the ruler under the presser foot from front to back. Very gently, by hand, turn the machine balance wheel to lower the needle towards the surface of the ruler just to touch (without scratching the ruler or damaging the needle) where the 0.75 cm (¼ in) mark is printed in from the right-hand edge of the ruler.

❸ Lower the presser foot to hold the ruler in this position. Check that it is running away from you at right angles by comparing a line on the ruler with a straight edge on the machine, such as the throat plate.

❹ Place a short length of masking tape on the machine against the right-hand edge of the ruler, as straight as possible. You will feed the fabric through touching this guide (**Diagram A**).

❺ You may need to make a cut or two into the masking tape, in order to open the throat plate to reach the bobbin.

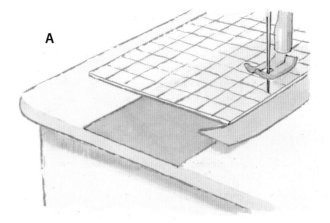

A

PREPARING TO SEW

1 Set up the machine on a stable surface. Also set up an iron and ironing board nearby. Always press patchwork as you go, before sewing across any seam again.

2 Put a new needle in the machine for each new project and thread the machine correctly.

3 Wind a bobbin with the chosen thread colour (two bobbins if it is a large project) and, when inserting the bobbin into the machine, check for any fluff around the bobbin case.

4 Using scraps of the fabrics to be sewn (two for regular piecing or including wadding if preparing to machine-quilt), work a short seam to test the tension. Adjust the tension if necessary.

PIECING

1 Put two patches, right sides together, with the raw edges level where you wish to join them.

2 Place the patches under the machine with the raw edges against your chosen guide, lower the presser foot and, with your right hand, hold the thread tails out of the way as you start sewing.

3 Sew as straight as you can, continuing beyond the edge of the patches, then stop.

4 If this is a single unit, lift the presser foot, pull the unit clear of the machine and cut the threads, leaving thread tails in the machine ready for the next task.

5 If this unit is one of a set, each to be worked the same, do not cut it free. Instead, continue to sew a little beyond the first unit, then feed in the next pair of patches to be joined together (**Diagram B**). Known as 'chain-piecing', this efficient method keeps all patches in the same batch together. When the end of the batch is reached, cut from the machine and press all the units before cutting apart.

PRESSING

Good pressing improves the look of the finished work immensely.

1 After stitching, press seams carefully. Use steam or dry as you prefer but always select the correct setting for the fabric type you are using.

2 Pieced seams are generally pressed to one side – usually towards the darker of the two fabrics so that the inlay is not seen. Pressing to one side makes a slight ridge that can help lock the patch to its neighbour at the next step, or to give an easy-to-follow edge for quilting 'in the ditch' later (see Machine-quilting, page 123).

3 Begin by pressing the unit exactly as sewn, in order to set the stitching. Then arrange the patch so that the seam allowances lie in the chosen direction and press a second time.

4 Turn the unit over and check the right side before moving on to the next one. If a patch is not pressed out fully, it will be smaller than intended when the next step is reached, or it may be distorted.

5 Compare the unit with the expected measurements. If making a large number of component parts for a project, you may want to check a random selection. However, if you have completed sewing a group of patches, each one should be checked before proceeding.

Note

If you come to quilt-making from dress-making, you will notice that the above instructions do not advise sewing backwards to secure the ends of the seams. It is not usual to do this when piecing, partly because it can get tedious but also because it can give a harder feel to the seam, often right where it will soon be stitched again. Providing the stitching starts before the leading fabric edge and continues beyond it into a little 'chain' of stitches, there is not usually any likelihood of the stitching pulling undone.

B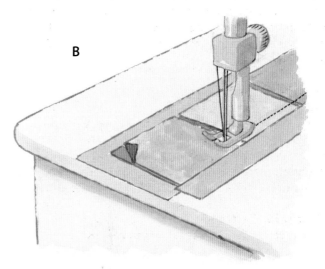

Appliqué

Although various methods exist for working appliqué, all of the projects featured in this book use fusible webbing to make the task easy, quick and durable. Make sure you buy a product that is suitable for finishing with zigzag or satin stitch, and read the product instructions before use to check the advised iron temperature and whether steam is required (see also, Materials, page 109).

FUSING

Make a sample before beginning your project:

❶ Draw or copy your motif to the correct size. You need to begin with it in reverse to the finished version, which can be achieved by turning it over on a white surface and drawing around the outline with a sharp pencil.

❷ Place the fusible webbing over the design, paper side up, and trace the shape on to the paper (**Diagram A**). Try to use the product economically by starting near one edge. Cut the shape out including a small margin.

❸ Place the appliqué fabric right side down on the ironing board, and position the cut-out motif on top, paper side up. Cover with nonstick baking parchment, if available. Use your iron to bond the motif on to the fabric then allow it to cool fully before handling, as the bond is not complete until cold.

❹ Using sharp embroidery scissors, cut out the motif carefully along the pencil lines.

❺ Peel off the paper backing. You can see that the fine webbing is now a slightly sticky film on the fabric. Position the motif correctly on the background fabric, sticky side down. Following the manufacturer's instructions closely, fuse the shape in place. Again, allow to cool before handling.

A

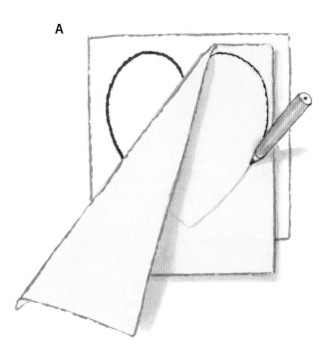

> **TIP**
> Keep an old tea towel handy to place on the ironing board when fusing and to avoid getting traces of webbing on the cover. A sheet of baking parchment placed over the work also prevents the accidental fusing of upside-down shapes to the iron.

FINISHING

Study your sewing-machine manual for advice on satin stitching and/or machine-embroidery. You may find that a specific 'open-toed' presser foot is recommended. This is designed to give you a good view of the 'line' you wish to stitch and also, perhaps, has a groove underneath to travel well over the stitching that has been worked. Set up the machine as directed for a fairly close zigzag or satin stitch.

Appliqué can be finished satisfactorily with regular sewing thread. However, if you have machine-embroidery threads, they can contribute more varied effects (see Materials, pages 108–109). Always test a new thread on a sample before sewing a block intended for a project. A common problem is stitching that bunches up like a bead – this means the stitch length is too short, in which case, increase it a little and try again.

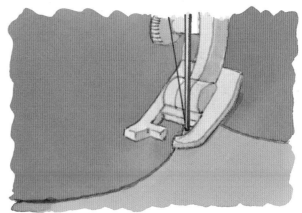

B

❶ Position the shape under the machine so that when the needle is at the right-hand side of its swing, it will pierce the background fabric right next to the applied motif (**Diagram B**). When it swings to the left, it should pass through both the appliqué and the background fabric behind it (**Diagram C**).

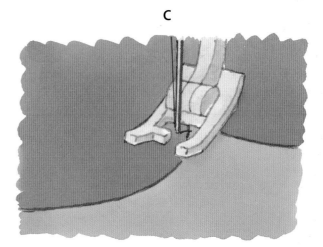

C

❷ To start sewing, manually rotate the balance wheel once to form a stitch and pull on the top thread to draw the bobbin thread to the top of the work. Holding both threads as you begin to sew avoids tangles underneath. Sew steadily to avoid distortion.

❸ You must plan where to start and stop sewing differently with different motifs. If there is an inside corner, such as the notch at the top of a heart, for example, this is a good place to begin because you can end your stitching just overlapping the start. At the end, without moving the work, raise the needle and select straight stitch again. Without changing the stitch length, sew two to three stitches to lock off the sewing. The top thread can be taken through to the reverse if desired and the ends tied for extra security.

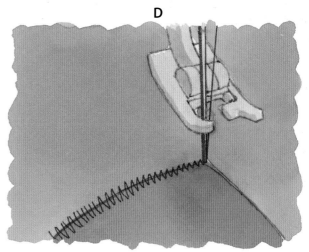

D

❹ When sewing curves, rotate the work gently, trying to maintain the closeness of the stitching around the outer edge. For corners, sew to the furthest point of the corner, stop with the needle in the fabric, lift the presser foot and turn the work for the new direction. Lower the presser foot and continue to sew (**Diagram D**).

❺ With composite motifs, you need to study the order in which to sew the parts for the best appearance. Always ensure the end of one outline is covered by the stitching of the next outline, to avoid having gaps.

Machine-embroidery

Patchwork and quilting are sometimes considered to be branches of embroidery, so it is not surprising to find that machine-embroidery is an increasing feature of quilt-making. When you have a line of stitching to sew on the machine, it can take scarcely any longer to select a machine-embroidery stitch to make the same line more interesting.

As some of the projects in this book rely on decorative stitches in the machine, it is worth familiarizing yourself with the stitches that your particular machine has to offer. Machines that can work zigzag stitch very often include a few basic variations on this, even if they do not have elaborate patterns.

BASIC GUIDELINES

• Study your machine manual to discover which stitches are available, whether there are special presser feet for embroidery, such as a free-machining or darning foot, and whether you can drop or cover the feed dogs in order to work freely. Even if this is not possible, there may still be ways to achieve the desired result.

• Often, machines perform embroidery better if the work is fixed in a hoop. Make sure, when buying a hoop for this task, that it is easy to slide under the presser foot of your machine. Embroidery stitches often tend to look better with another layer, such as a lightweight interfacing, behind the main fabric. This reduces any tendency to gather up the main fabric and can be trimmed back carefully to the stitching when completed.

• Set up your machine as the manual directs and make a sample before beginning on the actual project. Machine embroidery stitches, machine settings and threads are all very sensitive to small variations, especially in tension. (See also Equipment, pages 110–111.) You should also buy and use special machine-embroidery needles, which are particularly useful with metallic threads.

• When starting to sew, always lower the needle by hand into the starting point, turning the balance wheel fully to bring the needle back out again. Pull on the top thread to bring the bobbin thread to the surface so that you can hold both ends out of the way firmly when starting to sew. This prevents the threads becoming a 'bird's nest' on the back of the work or having the bobbin thread snarled around the bobbin case. Remember also to lower the presser foot.

• If you are new to machine embroidery, it is worth taking a piece of fabric mounted on iron-on interfacing and sewing a short length of each stitch pattern your machine offers. This gives a much better idea of appearance and scale than diagrams in a book and will help with future stitch selection.

SOME USEFUL STITCHES

Zigzag/satin stitch
This is most often used to finish appliqué motifs, and is used in some projects as a quilting stitch or for securing binding in place. It is also used when making decorative cords and to couch down yarns or ribbons. Generally, satin stitch is simply zigzag stitch worked more closely together, and, if you have a continuously variable control, interesting effects can be achieved by widening or narrowing the swing while sewing. Your machine may have a variation of this stitch that alternates between wide and narrow to give the appearance of a row of beads.

Blind-hem stitch
This variation of zigzag makes a fixed number of small straight stitches followed a single swing stitch and then repeats the sequence. When executed well, running close to a folded edge and with a minimal 'bite' into the fold, it can give the appearance of hand-sewing. In Love and Kisses (see pages 54–57), it is used to attach the sashing strips to the quilt-as-you-go blocks. It can also be used to couch yarns or ribbons and to finish bindings.

'Hand-quilting' stitch
Devised in response to the demands of quilt-makers, this stitch is available on newer machines and is intended to resemble hand-worked quilting.

Writing
Some sophisticated machines offer writing programmes, useful for making labels or to add decorative writing on sashings and borders.

Free-machine quilting/embroidery
For this technique, the machine feed is no longer driving the fabric through under the needle, but the user moves the work about freely instead. A hoop is generally required and interfacing, or even a piece

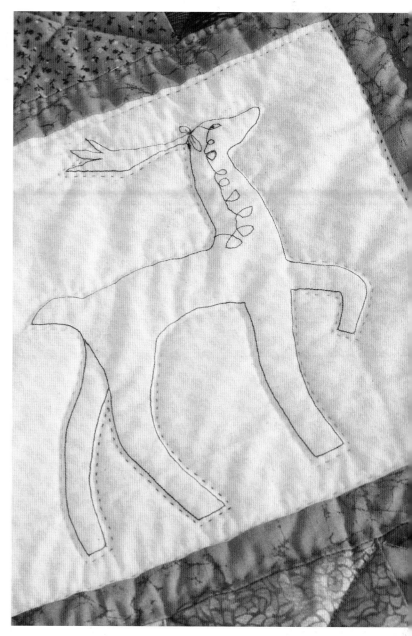

of tissue paper, below. Special feet are advised, but the presser foot lever must be lowered as usual in order to fully engage the stitch mechanism. This method can be used for writing quilt labels as well as 'drawing' designs with the machine, but it requires considerable practice to become competent. Take great care not to get your fingers under the needle.

Assembling the Quilt Top

A conventionally made quilt top may have blocks worked for the centre that can be joined directly to each other or with strips of fabric known as sashing. This centre may then be framed by one or more borders.

Instructions for joining blocks into rows or columns, adding sashing and attaching borders follow. Always begin by spreading out your blocks or panels the right way up, checking that you have the right number and making a pleasing arrangement. Set up your iron and press each step carefully.

JOINING BLOCKS IN ROWS

Blocks are commonly joined in horizontal rows. Pin a label to the first block in each row to help you keep track as you progress.

① Pick up the first two blocks in row 1, right sides together and match the raw edges for sewing together. Pin at right angles to your sewing line, starting by matching the centres together, then adding a pin at each corner (**Diagram A**). Add more pins, depending on the size of the blocks.

② Sew the seam, taking the planned 0.75 cm (¼ in) seam allowance.

③ Leave these two blocks in the machine, as for chaining patches together (see Patchwork techniques, page 115), and prepare the next two blocks, as above, for sewing together. Repeat until all blocks in the row are joined in pairs, although there may sometimes be an odd one.

④ Cut the first pair of blocks free and open them out to check that they are joined correctly. Check the next pair in the same way. Place these two pairs of blocks together, pinning as above, and sew.

JOINING BLOCKS IN COLUMNS

The process is basically the same as that for joining blocks into rows, except that you sew the bottom of the first block in row 1 to the top of the first block in row 2. Labelling the columns is useful for keeping track of the work.

JOINING BLOCKS WITH SASHING

Lay out the cut strips of sashing fabric between all of the blocks in your layout, just as it should look in the final quilt. Start with the first block in row or column 1. Following the pinning notes above (Step 1, Joining blocks in rows), pin a sashing strip to the appropriate edge of the block (**Diagram B**) then sew and press. Repeat, adding sashing to each block in the same row. Check the seams before joining these units together in pairs, as in step 4, above. Press the seams towards the sashing.

Several projects require you to make up rows or columns of units in this way, which are then sewn to quilt-as-you-go layers (see Quilting techniques, page 125).

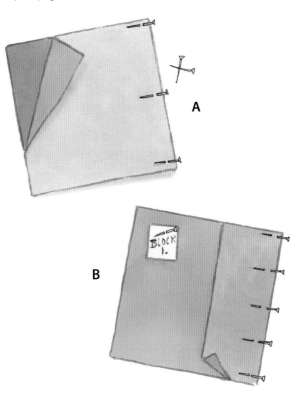

A

B

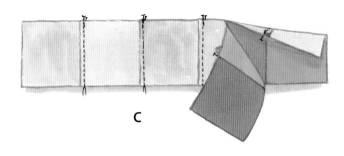

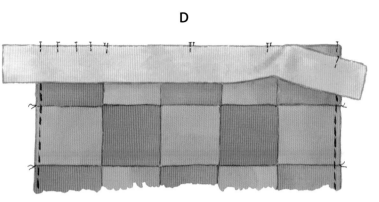

D

JOINING ROWS OF BLOCKS

For a conventional quilt top, check that the rows are joined in the correct sequence then continue as follows:

❶ With the first two rows or columns right sides together, pin to match together the seams on both rows, whether with or without sashing, and the centres of the blocks. Bring together and match the ends of the rows, and pin. Add pins between as necessary, especially where there are points or seams that need to meet up exactly (**Diagram C**).

❷ Sew the seam carefully. Remove from the machine and check whether the matches are as good as you wish before pressing and proceeding to the next pair of rows or columns. With large projects, it is more convenient to assemble the top into halves or thirds, instead of sewing each pair of rows to the previous pair each time.

ATTACHING BORDERS

When the top is assembled, measure across the centre either vertically or horizontally to check how long the first borders need to be. (Do not measure at the edges, as they are often stretchy and can seem to be longer.) The border strip lengths in the projects in this book include extra fabric as 'insurance' – that is, they are all 5–7.5 cm (2–3 in) longer than the required amount to allow for any inaccuracies that creep in when making the blocks. Note also that side borders are often a different length from those at the top and bottom.

❶ Transfer the quilt-top measurement on to one long edge of the relevant border strip.

❷ Fold the measured border length in half (short ends together), and then quarters and mark with pins. Divide the appropriate edge of the quilt in the same way. Now unfold each and place the two edges

together, pinning at right angles, and matching points on the patch edges to the stitching line as necessary (**Diagram D**).

❸ Sew carefully, keeping the seam allowances as pressed when sewing over them. Check the fit and press the seams towards the borders before trimming the excess length. Repeat for the other matching border.

❹ Now measure the quilt in the opposite direction to check the length for the remaining borders. Repeat steps 1, 2 and 3 to attach these borders to the remaining two edges of the quilt.

Quilting

Quilting is the stitching that holds the three layers of the quilt together. Although the projects in this book are machine-quilted for speed, there are several where you may choose to hand-quilt if you have time and want to give it a try. Quilting motifs are usually marked, where necessary, before the top is layered.

The projects in this book are quilted in one of two ways. For the traditional method, a top layer is assembled, layered together with wadding and backing fabric, and then quilted. Alternatively, the backing fabric and wadding are put together and the top layer is worked by stitching through these two layers, thus quilting at the same time as joining the parts. This latter technique is termed 'quilt-as-you-go' and the projects include variations that allow you to work in blocks or sections.

TRADITIONAL QUILTING

Each project has instructions for working the quilt top. Spread the wadding out somewhere to recover from its packaging at the same time as you begin working the top. When the top is complete, press it and check the reverse side for stray threads, which should be snipped away, not pulled out.

Backing fabric

Fabric for backing should be light enough in colour not to show through the quilt. Small all-over patterns are popular, especially for beginners, as they hide inequalities of stitch. Many quilters choose prints to suit the theme of a quilt; alternatively, they piece together a number of leftovers to construct the required area.

The backing should be at least 10–15 cm (4–6 in) larger than the quilt top. The quilt size may mean that the backing has to be joined. You may have to decide exactly how to do this yourself, depending on your fabric. Sew any joins, taking a 2 cm (¾ in) seam, trim away both selvedges and press the seam open. A single join can run vertically or horizontally but should avoid coinciding with a major construction seam on the quilt top. Another method is to sew two lengths of backing right sides together down both edges to make a tube. Refold so that the seams lie on top of each other and cut one of the long folded edges to give a central panel with a half-width on each side. It

may also be possible to buy wider fabric, such as plain muslin, or to use sheeting. Press the backing fabric before layering.

Assembling quilt layers

Before you start, prepare a large, clean surface, such as the floor, for working on.

❶ Spread out the backing on your surface, right side down. Secure the edges at intervals either with pieces of masking tape (if to hard flooring) or pins (to carpet).

❷ Centre the wadding over the backing and smooth out without stretching or distorting it.

❸ With the right side up, centre the completed quilt top over the wadding. If you do not position it correctly at first, lift it and try again. Do not drag it about, however, as this will disturb the wadding below. A tip with a large project is to fold the top lightly into quarters and place with the centre corner to the centre of the wadding before unfolding the quilt top over the rest.

❹ The three layers must be basted together thoroughly to avoid problems while quilting. Either baste with thread, using a large needle such as a 'straw', if available, and starting with a large knot; alternatively use safety pins. Baste in a grid, starting at the centre and working outwards vertically and horizontally.

Spray-glue basting

Many quilting suppliers sell aerosol cans of temporary fabric glue, which speed the task of layering. This glue is also popular for machine-quilting because there is much less risk of any layer shifting against the others. Read the manufacturer's instructions for safe use and follow them closely. It will be necessary to spray twice, once to stick together the backing and wadding, and again to stick the quilt top to the wadding. The product allows for some repositioning if you discover any slight wrinkles. No other thread- or pin-basting should be required. The product disperses after a while so it is sensible to layer and quilt within a short space of time. If you suspect that any glue remains by the time you want to use or give away the quilt, you can wash it to remove any last traces.

Machine-quilting

If this is your first attempt at machine-quilting, make a practice sample before starting on the quilt proper. Use a 30 cm (12 in) square of pieced fabric, wadding and backing and follow the procedure below.

1 Prepare your sewing machine as advised for piecing, except that if you have a walking foot, fit it instead of the regular foot. Carry out a tension test with the type of wadding you have chosen. You may also find that reducing the downward pressure on the presser foot causes less movement between the layers.

2 Set the stitch length control to '0'. Place your work under the machine, lower the presser foot and turn the balance wheel by hand to insert the needle where you wish to start. Continue turning the wheel to bring the needle back out of the fabric. Now pull on the top thread tail to bring up the bobbin thread to the top of the work.

3 Hold both thread tails (to avoid them becoming tangled) and run the machine very briefly, making just two to three stitches on the spot. This saves sewing in the thread ends afterwards: they can simply be threaded into a needle for carrying into the quilt layers.

4 Return to the stitch length you want and start sewing, following the pieced seams or a drawn line. Try to sew steadily. Having your fingers each side of the seam, pulling very slightly to open up the seam a little, can help to keep the stitching well 'in-the-ditch'.

5 At the end of the seam or design line, return the stitch length to '0' and sew two to three stitches to lock the end. Raise the presser foot and either remove the work from the machine entirely or move to the next part to be stitched. Cut the sewing thread, leaving enough to thread into a needle for hiding in the quilt layers.

6 To change direction at a corner, first lower the needle into the work at the corner. Lift the presser foot and turn the work as required. Lower the presser foot again before resuming sewing. However, it is generally not advisable to keep changing direction, sewing back and forth, which can cause an effect known as 'sheering'. This is when ripples

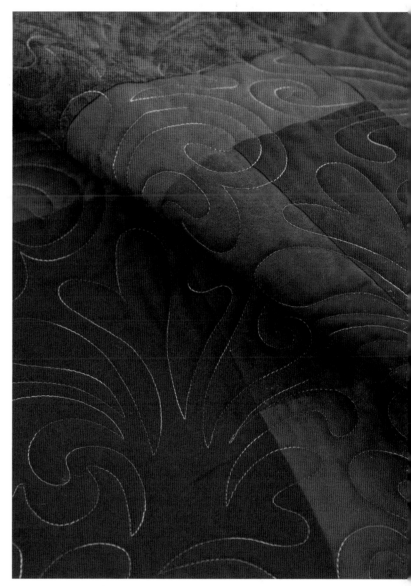

appear on the quilt surface where the top layer has travelled in opposite directions across the wadding during stitching. For the best results, start at the same end of the quilt when sewing the main lines of a pattern.

7 With large projects, managing the body of the quilt while sewing can be a challenge. Roll or fold lightly to feed under the arm of the machine. Support the extra weight perhaps with an ironing board set up beside the machine table.

Hand-quilting

If you like hand-sewing, you will probably enjoy hand-quilting. Some projects suggest a combination of techniques: machine-quilting the basic structure of the quilt first, then highlighting parts, such as appliqué motifs, with a line of hand-quilting. This is a great way to try hand-quilting without having to take on the job of marking a design.

Hand-quilting is usually worked in quilting thread, which is stronger than sewing cotton and generally waxed for sliding through the layers smoothly. Hand-sewing needles called 'betweens' or 'quilting' needles are used. A beginner should buy a pack of assorted sizes and take the time to experiment with them. As you grow in skill, smaller needles can be used to achieve smaller stitches.

However, evenness, in the form of even stitch size and even tension, is more important than size for a pleasing appearance. Avoid pulling the thread too tightly because the effect of hand-quilting results just from the compression of the wadding between the outer fabrics. The line of stitching should not feel taut and hard within the quilt layers.

Begin with a small knot and pull this firmly until it pops inside the layers. Then work running stitch through all the layers until you reach the end of either the design line or the thread (**Diagram A**). Wind the thread around the needlepoint once (**Diagram B**) and insert the needlepoint where the last stitch goes (**Diagram C**). Pull the needle through elsewhere and listen for that last knot popping into the layers. Keep slight tension on the thread as you snip it off so that it also slides back into the layers.

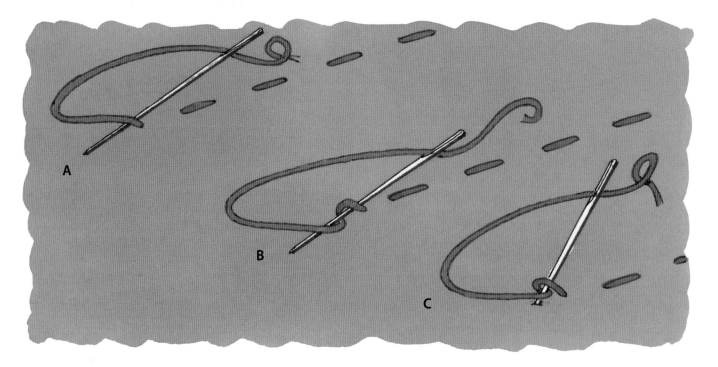

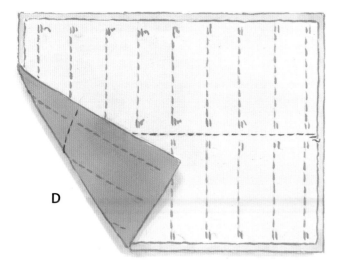

D

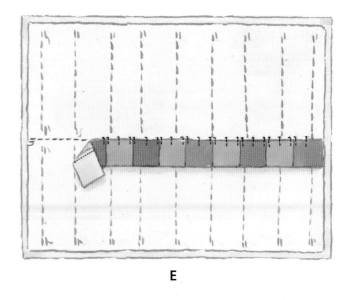

E

QUILT-AS-YOU-GO

There are two basic methods for quilting as-you-go: the 'entire-quilt' method and the 'unit' method.

Entire-quilt method

For this method, you need to start with backing fabric that is 10–15 cm (4–6 in) larger than the intended size of the final quilt, joined if necessary.

1 Lay the backing fabric out flat, right side down.

2 Centre the wadding on top of the backing fabric (low-loft or needle-punched wadding suit quilt-as-you-go projects).

3 Baste the two layers together. Do not use safety pins, which could break the machine needle if overlooked. Consider the direction in which you will be sewing most of the piecing and insert thread-basting at right angles to this.

4 For some projects you will need to insert a straight baseline of basting to guide the placing of the piecing. If this is the case, use a different colour thread (**Diagram D**).

5 Usually, strips of piecing are worked on the machine to an appropriate length and pressed before sewing to the quilt layers. Place the first strip, right side up, along the placement line. Pin at right angles

to the seam and baste (**Diagram E**). Place the next strip right sides to the first with raw edges level and pin through all the layers. Machine-sew, taking a 0.75 cm (¼ in) seam allowance, removing the pins as you go. Use a walking foot if you have one.

6 Flip the second strip right side up and lightly press the seam, setting the iron at a reduced temperature, such as 'cool' or 'wool' instead of the usual 'cotton'. Avoid direct contact between the iron and the wadding by using a press cloth over areas not yet covered by fabric.

7 Pin the edge of the second strip in place at right angles to the seam, ready for adding the third strip.

8 Repeat the process until the whole surface is covered. Trim the edges of the quilt to straighten, then bind (see Finishing a quilt, pages 126–128). Remove the basting threads from the back of the quilt.

Unit method

Large quilts can be challenging to handle but quilt-as-you-go makes them easier to complete by allowing you to work either just a number of blocks or sections of the whole at any one time. You can then join the separate units using extra strips of fabric to neaten the joins. They can appear as decorative sashing on both front and back (see Love and Kisses, pages 54–57, or Liberated Log Cabin, pages 26–31) or just on the back, when they are cut from the same fabric. Specific directions for joining accompany each project.

Finishing a Quilt

Several methods exist for finishing the edges of a quilt. Two of the most useful are described here because they suit the projects in this book.

The first method, binding, suits the majority of projects, particularly those worked with quilt-as-you-go. It is practical and offers a good opportunity to add to the design, perhaps with a bold or dark colour or an interesting fabric. The second method is known by various names, among them, 'edge-to-edge'. This method is often seen on old quilts and involves turning in the edges of both the backing and the top to enclose the trimmed-to-size wadding. The edge can be sewn invisibly by hand, machine top-stitched or hand-quilted, in this case often with two parallel rows of stitching.

BINDING

Binding can be cut either straight or on the bias. Straight binding suits many quilts and is stable to sew. Bias binding is needed for curved edges and can create interesting effects, such as when striped or checked fabric is used. Binding need not be made of the same fabric for all its length. The following instructions suit any width of binding.

Preparing the edges of the quilt
Insert a line of thread-basting (by hand or machine) within the seam allowance, so that the layers will behave as one when you attach the binding. This remains in place and will stabilize the edge if ever the binding needs replacing.

Preparing the binding strips
Follow the project instructions for the finished width of the binding, or decide on a finished width of your own. There must be at least enough wadding and backing to come right to the folded edge of the binding, even if it contains only the minimum seam allowance from the quilt top.

❶ To determine the cut width required, multiply the finished width of the binding by four and add 0.25 cm (1/8 in) for ease.

❷ To determine the length of binding to cut, three calculations must be added together: the total distance along the sides of quilt; an extra amount for making the four mitred corners; plus an extra amount for joining the tails (see below). Make the calculation for the mitred corners by multiplying the finished width of the binding by eight. As the tails are joined diagonally, make the calculation here by multiplying the cut (not finished) width by three. For narrow bindings, finishing less than 2.5 cm (1 in) wide, an additional 25–30 cm (10–12 in) should be enough for mitring corners and joining the ends.

❸ Cut the binding strips from ironed fabric using the rotary cutter.

Joining the strips
❶ Place two strips, right sides together, overlapping their ends at right angles. Fold down the end of the top strip to touch the side and crease lightly (**Diagram A**). Unfold, then sew along the crease with matching thread and using a short stitch length on the machine (**Diagram B**).

❷ Check that the join is correct by opening the strip out (**Diagram C**). Press the seam open and trim to 0.5 cm (scant 1/4 in). Repeat the process until the desired length is achieved.

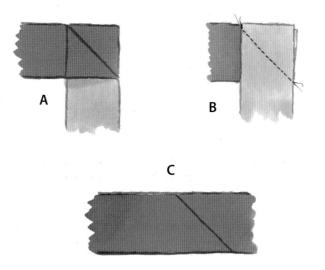

A

B

C

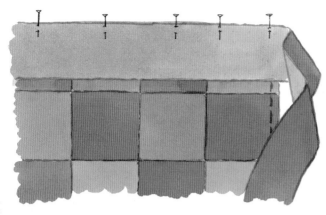

C

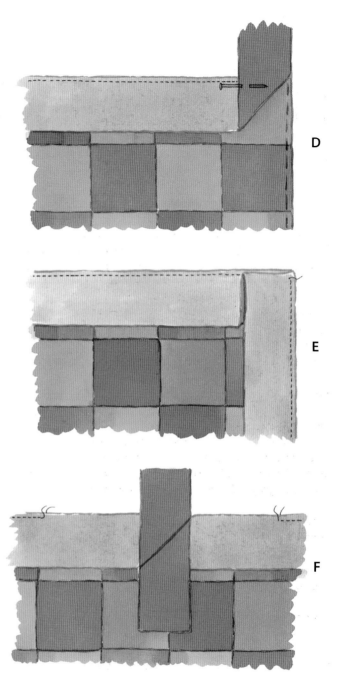

D

E

F

Continuous binding with automatic mitres

This method attaches a continuous length of binding to a quilt by sewing one side at a time.

❶ Starting part way along one side and leaving a tail for joining later, pin the binding to the top side of the quilt as far as the first corner (**Diagram C**). Insert the last pin as far from the corner as the finished binding width will be. Sew carefully, removing pins as you go, and stop exactly at the last pin. Sew backwards for a few stitches. Remove the quilt from the machine and cut the threads.

❷ To fold the corner mitre, start by making a crease in the binding just where the edge of the quilt is. Lift the binding upwards at right angles to the quilt edge so that this crease aligns with the top edge of the quilt, forming a diagonal fold in the binding (**Diagram D**). Now fold the binding down at the crease so that it runs level with the side of the quilt to which it will be sewn next (**Diagram E**). Do not skimp on this fold.

❸ Pin the binding in place as far as the next corner, exactly as before. Stitch as far as the last pin, reverse-sew and cut free.

❹ Fold the second corner mitre as above and pin, then sew to the third side. Repeat the process to turn the third corner and the fourth.

❺ After turning the fourth corner, pin and sew the last side only part way towards where you began, leaving a gap of about 25–30 cm (10–12 in) for joining the ends.

❻ To join the ends so they match existing joins, lay the two tails along the edge of the quilt where they will lie. Halfway between, fold one tail at right angles above the quilt and the other at the same point at right angles towards the quilt centre (**Diagram F**). (The rotary cutting ruler can be used to achieve a right angle.) Crease each one lightly, then match the crease carefully, right sides together, and sew, keeping the rest of the quilt clear of the stitching. Check the fit of the join along the quilt side. If it is good, lightly press the seam open and trim the tails.

❼ Pin this joined section in place and sew.

❽ To complete, lightly press the binding right side up away from the quilt surface. Fold the binding to the back of the quilt, turn in the raw edge and sew in place either by hand or by machine.

Double binding

With projects such as Coffee and Cream (see pages 78–81) that use silk fabric, which frays readily, it is definitely easier to use double binding. The method for attaching double binding is the same as for attaching single binding, along the following lines.

1 Determine the desired finished width visible on the front of the quilt, say 1 cm (³⁄₈ in), multiply by six and add 0.25 cm (¹⁄₈ in) for ease. Cut strips to achieve the required length as described on page 126.

2 Join the binding strips as above then fold them accurately in half, right side out, and press.

3 When attaching, leave a longer tail unattached at the start because it must be opened out to a single layer for a neat join at the end.

Proceed to pin and sew the binding to the quilt, one side at a time and folding the mitres carefully as above.

4 When pinning the last section, approaching where you began, leave a larger gap between the ends than for single binding – at least 30 cm (12 in) or more for wider bindings.

5 Unfold the binding to a single layer and join the ends as above. Check the fit before pressing and trimming. Replace the fold, pin, and sew the final section to cover the gap.

6 Lightly press the binding away from the quilt centre then turn it to the back of the quilt and sew the folded edge in place to the existing line of stitching either by hand or by machine.

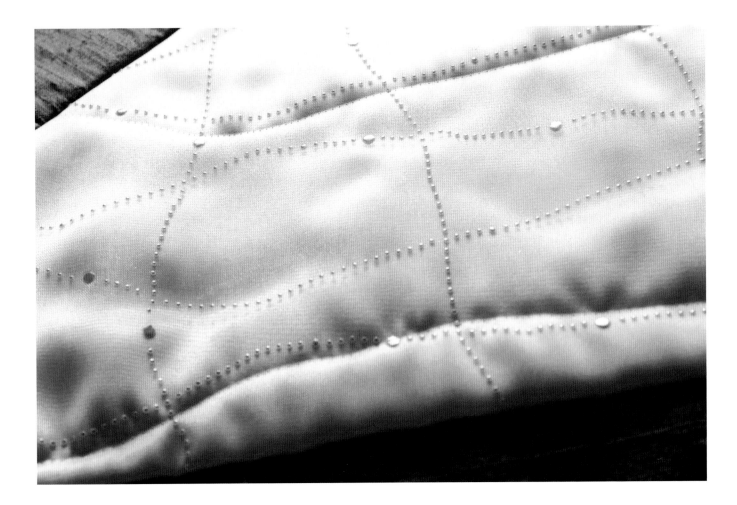

EDGE-TO-EDGE FINISHING

This method can be used only in certain circumstances: when the quilting does not yet run right to the edges of the quilt, and when there is enough fabric beyond the intended finished edge to allow a modest seam allowance on the quilt top and the backing. If appropriate, the edge can be finished and the quilting completed up to the edge.

① Trim the layers carefully and individually: the wadding to the exact desired final size; the top and backing fabrics to include 2 cm (³⁄₄ in) extra on all sides for turnings. If you wish, either the top or the backing could have slightly more or less turning. In this case, it would be sensible to keep the wider turning on the darker fabric to avoid the shadow of a dark layer projecting beyond the light turning.

② Fold one of the layers to enclose the trimmed edge of the wadding, mitring and trimming the corners as necessary, and baste in place.

③ Fold and pin the other layer, checking that it will be level with the edge already prepared. Mitre and trim corners and baste through all the layers (**Diagram G**).

④ Sew the layers together either by hand, invisibly slip-stitching the folds together with sewing thread, or using quilting thread and stitches close to the edge (and perhaps again, parallel) or by machine, either a single row of stitching or two rows with a narrow even space between.

MAKING A HANGING SLEEVE

① Cut a length of fabric as long as the quilt is wide, and 24–25 cm (9¹⁄₂–10 in) deep. This fabric can be a spare piece of the chosen backing or something else, such as calico.

② On both short ends, press 1 cm (³⁄₈ in) to the wrong side, twice, forming a hem, and machine-sew in place.

③ Fold the sleeve in half lengthwise, right sides out, and sew, taking a 1.25 cm (¹⁄₂ in) seam allowance. Refold the tube of fabric created so that the seam is centred and can be pressed open.

④ Place the seam side of the tube to the back of the quilt at the top and centred across the width of the quilt. Hand-sew in place.

Note

If the quilt is very big, make the sleeve in the same manner but divide it into two lengths so that the hanging pole can be supported in the middle.

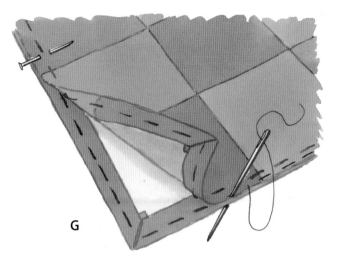

G

Labels

- It is worth labelling your quilts, at the very least with your name and the date the quilt was completed. You might also add the quilt name, where you live and a dedication – especially if the quilt is a gift for a celebration, such as a wedding or a special birthday. You may own a machine that will embroider writing for you; if not, labels can be handwritten using pens and markers produced specifically for writing on fabric. You can also write in pencil to embroider over by hand or machine. Light fabrics make this task easier, and quilting shops often sell labels printed on pretty fabric with space for writing a personal message.

- Rough out what you wish to say, laying it out in pencil over lined or graph paper until you are happy with the appearance. Ink it over so that you can read it through your fabric when placed on top. Trace and either ink with a fabric pen or embroider. Press under a narrow turning all around and sew to the back of the quilt, usually at the bottom.

Customizing and Variations

All of the projects in this book offer variations on the basic instructions, sometimes in very small ways and occasionally more radically. The intention is to encourage you to personalize your quilts and to emphasize that quilt-making is a creative activity: it is not necessary to copy the exact appearance of the quilts in the pictures.

There are four basic ways in which you can deviate from the original: by using different fabrics; by choosing a different colour scheme; by changing the size of the project or by replacing the design elements with some of your own.

USING DIFFERENT FABRICS

It is quite likely that your fabrics will be at least a little different because fabrics change every season. Rather than being a problem, this provides the opportunity to make your own choices for substitutes.

CHANGING THE COLOUR SCHEME

To aim for an entirely different colour scheme may be a bigger step but often has a starting point, say, in the existing decor of a bedroom. This effectively rules out all other colour families, so simplifies things to a degree. However, just because you might want a blue version of Take a Bite (see pages 82–85), it does not mean that a single shade of blue is the answer. Effective colour schemes usually contain a range of values (light and dark), though both extremes are not always needed. Very often, a colour scheme benefits from an accent of something unexpected: a bright among many soft or dark shades, for example.

Some mail-order fabric shops offer sample swatches that are useful for working out alternative colour schemes. When forming a scheme, use patches for the dominant fabrics and swatches for the accent colours.

CHANGING THE SIZE

Small adjustments in size might be the result of a slight error in construction or because slightly less fabric was available. For example, with Bright Kites (see pages 100–105), you might see 'the perfect sky' – an end-of-roll and marked down in price, but 10 cm (4 in) shorter than required. This would not make much difference to the end result.

Certain projects adapt more readily than others. The Hit 'n' Miss variations are very flexible, for example (see pages 18–21): simply choose a new length or width and, if necessary, adjust the width of the edge strips. Projects with rows of blocks can be resized either by changing the block size or by adding or subtracting rows. If adding more rows, you must calculate how much more fabric you will need. Besides checking the block size to see how much more length is required, you must also determine how many units can be cut from the fabric width. A single extra row of blocks may cut into more than one width of fabric. Clearly the same question must also be asked if changing the block size. When enlarging a project, if in doubt always round up to the nearest 50 cm (½ yd), as leftovers will add to your stash.

REPLACING DESIGN ELEMENTS

This might sound more challenging than the options above, but the result is a much more personal end product. A simple solution would be to take ideas from two or three projects and combine them. As an example, the basic method of the Hit 'n' Miss quilt – organizing fabrics into light and dark values – could use blocks from Katharine's Stars (see pages 22–25) simply by adjusting the larger strip width to accommodate the star blocks. You could put bright stars with dark sky in the dark strips and either no stars in the light strips or dark stars with light sky. With the Winter Wonderland quilt structure (see pages 86–89), you could replace the reindeer and trees with either free-machined drawings of the patterns from Ice-cream Sundae (see pages 68–71) or with appliqué blocks exactly as directed. Frame them to size in the same way and set them with colourful summery fabrics. If wishing to make a quilt to please a particular person, a wide variety of copyright-free images exist on the Internet, which could be simplified to suit appliqué techniques.

However tentatively you make your first attempts at personalizing a project, the reward will be the joy of an individual interpretation and, with it, greater confidence to make braver decisions in future.

Caring for Quilts

If a quilt is used on a bed or sofa, the chances are that it will need laundering. Dry cleaning is only recommended for wall hangings such as those made with silk or other special fibres because fumes may remain in the fibres, and so would not be suitable for bedding.

WASHING AND CLEANING

It is sensible to wash fabrics before using them to make quilts. The exception to this are silks or other special fabrics where the end product is a wall hanging. Quilts designed for bedding or some other useful purpose ought to be made with washable wadding. Check the manufacturer's product-care instructions to be sure that you select a wadding appropriate for the intended use, and follow these instructions when washing the quilt. Regular polyester waddings are washable.

Always use the coolest possible water temperature, whether washing by hand or machine, to reduce the likelihood of loose colour washing out of dark fabrics and cross-staining lighter areas. A gentle colour-safe washing product helps preserve the original fabric colours.

If using a machine, choose a minimum, gentle wash cycle with a short spin. Small quilts may be dried in a tumble dryer (subject to wadding care notes), on low heat. Remove before fully dry and spread out flat to finish drying to reduce creasing. If quilts are dried outdoors, a clean sheet placed over the top can reduce fading in sunlight.

Hand-washing a quilt of any size requires care, particularly if it is very large. Quilts can be laundered in the bath, where the same rules apply about washing products and temperature. Do not wring or twist during washing or rinsing. Several rinses will be required involving a large amount of water at each stage. Having absorbed a lot of water, the quilt will be very heavy – even if you have pressed out as much as you can – and this can cause sewing threads to break. Use a clean sheet or towel like a hammock to lift the quilt out into a waterproof container (as it will still be very wet). Place it on colourfast towels and squeeze out as much water as possible before drying flat.

WALL HANGINGS

Wall hangings collect a surprising amount of dust, and benefit from being taken down and shaken outdoors, or from a light vacuum if more permanently fixed to the wall. A pair of old tights over the suction tube allows dust to past through while reducing the risk of removing embellishments too.

SUN DAMAGE

The industry term 'light fast' covers relatively few hours and, for this reason, you should avoid placing wall hangings in direct sunlight at any time of day. This is not always possible with a bed quilt, however. To slow down the effects of sun damage, try to keep the curtains closed during the part of the day when the sun strikes the bed. Choosing an all-over, multi-directional design allows you to rotate a quilt that receives a lot of sun, so evening out wear as well as sun damage. An alternative strategy for both walls and beds is to have several items (perhaps themed to the seasons) so that one can be in use or on show while others have a rest.

STORING

The ideal is to keep quilts as flat as possible, so unless you have regular visitors, placing a few on a spare bed with a sheet over the top for protection against light and dust could be a sound solution. If the stack grows, rearrange it regularly so that the same quilts are not always at the bottom, squashed by the weight of those on top.

The next best alternative is to roll the quilt around a large-diameter cardboard tube (such as used for carpet). Cover the tube first with acid-free tissue and roll with the right side of the quilt outwards then wrap in a clean sheet. Large quilts needing long tubes can possibly be stored under a bed. If the only option is to fold a quilt, fold it right side out, placing plenty of acid-free tissue along the folds. Refold the quilt differently at regular intervals.

Do not keep quilts in airing cupboards, where the atmosphere is too dry, nor in plastic bags, where they may become mouldy.

Transferring Designs

There are a number of ways to transfer a design on to a quilt. In some cases, it is a question of using a template that has to be enlarged before being transferred on to the fabric.

ENLARGING DESIGNS

The simplest method for enlarging templates, patterns and designs is to use a photocopier with an enlarging facility. If a design has been reduced by 50 per cent (that is half size) you will have to enlarge it by 200 per cent (double the size) to get it to the correct measurement for your design.

SQUARING UP

If you do not have access to a photocopier, you can enlarge a design by squaring up. This is a simple and reliable method that has been used by artists and designers for centuries. Draw a grid of 1.25 cm (½ in) squares over the motif to be enlarged, and plot a new grid on a plain sheet of paper, enlarging the squares by the same amount by which you wish to enlarge the motif. For example, if you want the motif four times bigger, your larger squares need to be 5 cm (2 in) square. Transfer the motif by drawing, freehand, what you see in each small square to the equivalent larger square.

TRANSFERRING MARKINGS

Once you have a pattern or motif enlarged to the correct size, there are a number of methods you can use to transfer it to the fabric for cutting out, embroidering or quilting. (See Marking supplies, page 111.)

To cut out shapes for patchwork or appliqué, use your pattern to make a template then draw the design on the back of your fabric in pencil. Bear in mind that, when working on the back of fabric, asymmetrical motifs need to be reversed.

To embroider simple designs (such as heart shapes), you can transfer the design to the fabric by drawing around a template on the front of the fabric using a vanishing marker. More complex embroidery designs need more detail, and the easiest way to transfer them is to use a light box. First trace or photocopy the design on to thin paper (such as tracing paper, typing paper or layout paper). Place the tracing on the light box and lay the pressed fabric over the top, right side up (if applicable). Ensure the motif is in the correct position and then trace it using a vanishing fabric marker or pencil.

Templates

Many quilting projects require special shapes, and the projects in this book are no exception. You can buy ready-made templates of standard shapes in quilting shops, but it is quite simple to make your own using card or plastic (see below). The templates for the projects in this book are shown at actual size unless a percentage enlargement is given (see Transferring designs, left).

MAKING TEMPLATES

• Accuracy is essential when making templates: they must be drawn around, cut out and used precisely.

• Thick card is acceptable for making templates that will be used only once or twice. Old cereal packets are fine.

• You can cut window templates from card, which allow you to see the pattern on the fabric for selective cutting; the card frame should be the exact size of the finished shape, plus seam allowance.

• Paper is useful for very large pieced shapes and big appliqué templates.

• Template plastic is firm, clear acetate that is durable and accurate for continued use. The advantage is that you can see through it for selective cutting and you can easily trace designs on to it using a fine permanent marker pen. For speed and accuracy, you can also buy template plastic with a grid printed on it from quilting shops. Keep plastic templates away from a hot iron.

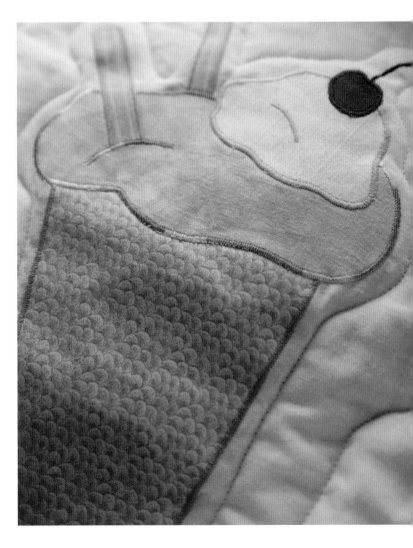

Stripy Fish

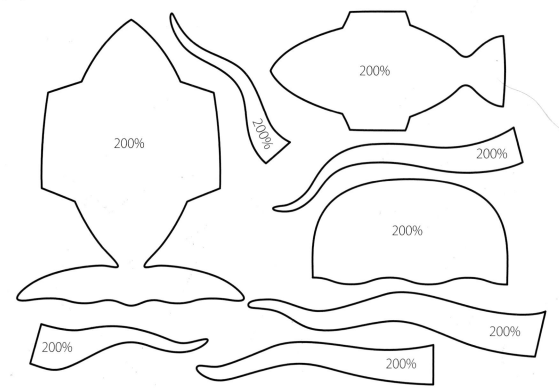

200%

200%

200%

200%

200%

200%

200%

200%

Stripy Fish

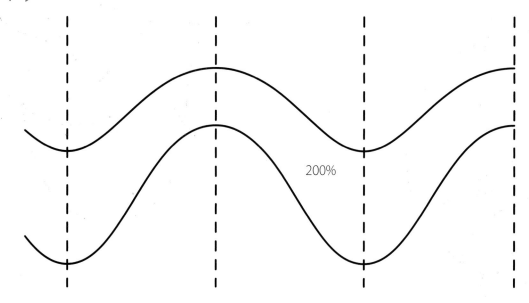

200%

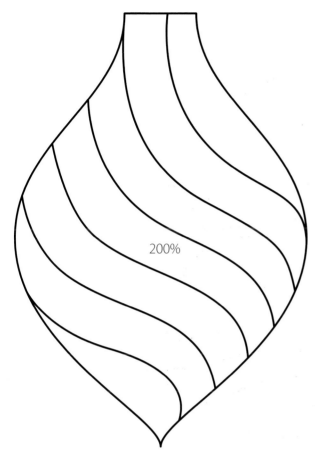

200%

Christmas Baubles

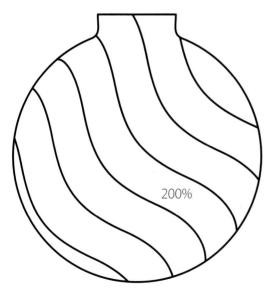

200%

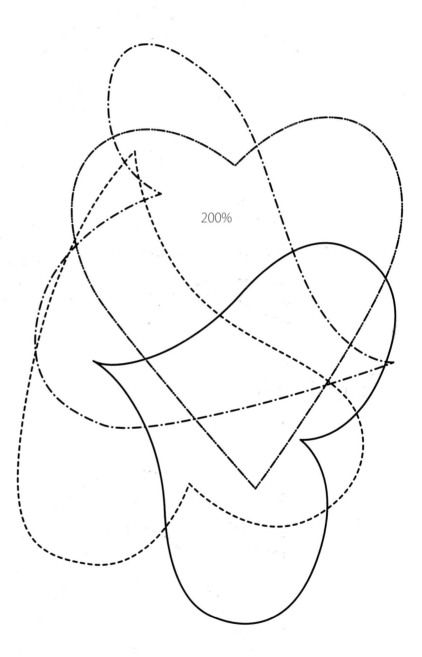

200%

Dieters' Dream

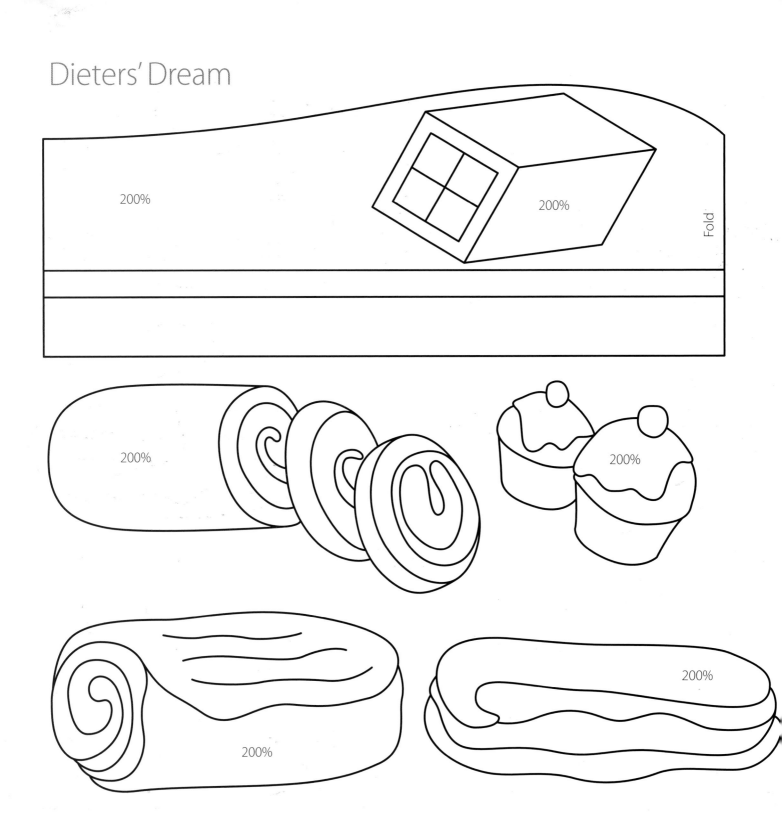

200%

200%

Fold

200%

200%

200%

200%

200%

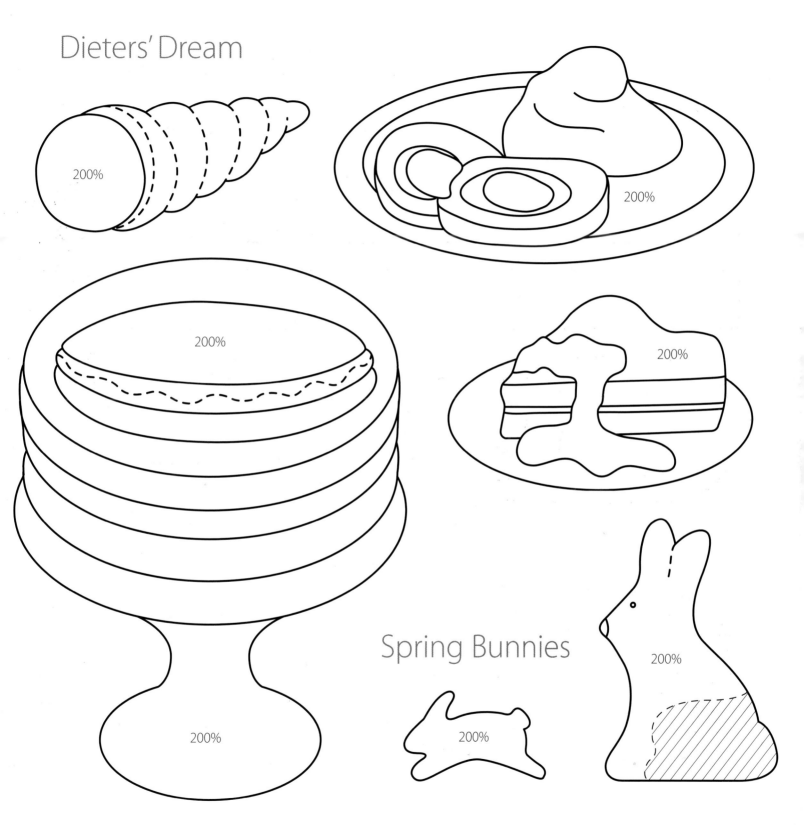

Dieters' Dream

200%

200%

200%

200%

200%

Spring Bunnies

200%

200%

Ice-cream Sundae

Ice-cream Sundae

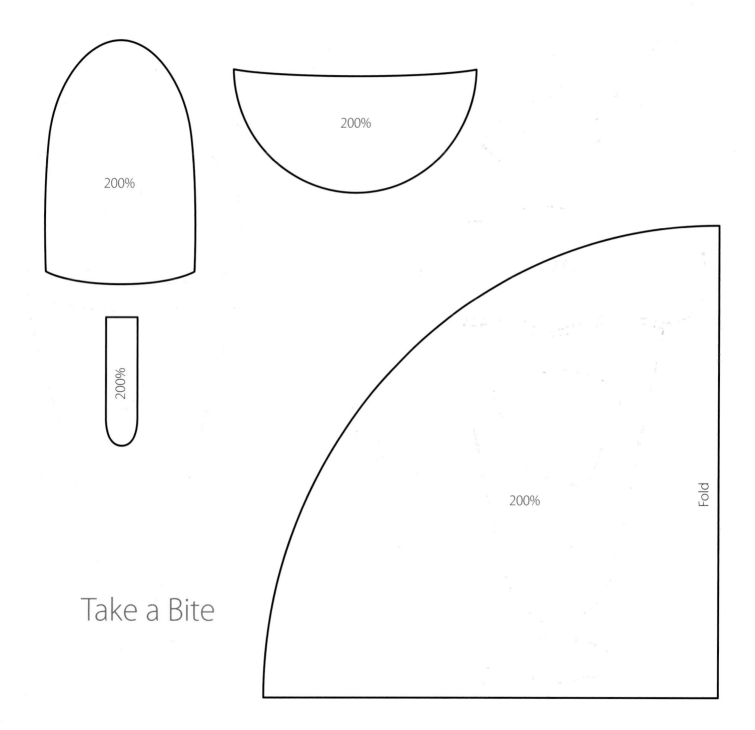

200%

200%

200%

Take a Bite

200%

Fold

200%

Winter Wonderland

200%

200%

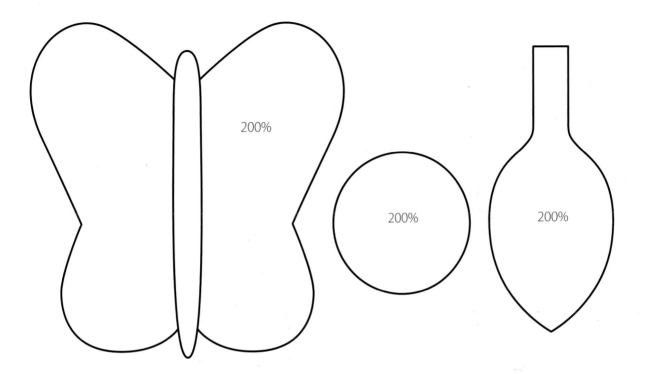

200%

200%

200%

Spencer's Sunflowers

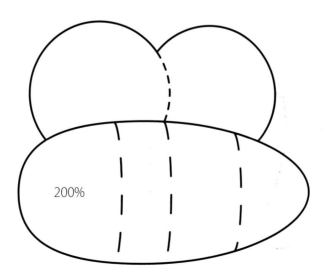

200%

Index

Acknowledgements

The makers of the quilts in this book would be delighted if their work inspired you to create your own interpretation rather than copying the projects exactly. However, if you enter such a quilt in a show, especially a competition, it is appropriate to mention the person or the book that prompted your work when filling in the entry form.

The author and publisher would like to thank the quilters who created the quilts for the projects in this book.

Cadeaux de Provence Therese Lauze and Jenni Dobson
Steamers Ahoy! Jill Cawrey
Hit 'n' Miss Sheila Pearson
Katherine's Stars Katharine Guerrier
Liberated Log Cabin Doreen Hallett
Stripey Fish Louise Wasilewski
Country Dance Jenni Last
Chedworth Evergreen Alix Ashurst and Jenni Dobson
Christmas Baubles Minou Button-De Groote
Love and Kisses Kay Anderson
Dieters' Dream Irene Nowell
Spring Bunnies Carol Dennis
Ice-cream Sundae Margaret Bates
Memento Magic Sue Atkinson
Coffee and Cream Margaret Bates
Take a Bite Veronika Smith
Winter Wonderland Judith Gill
Enchanted Forest Gill Tanner
Spencer's Sunflowers Louise Wasilewski
Bright Kites Jenni Dobson

Executive Editor Katy Denny
Editor Charlotte Wilson
Executive Art Editor Joanna MacGregor
Designer Beverly Price, One2six
Photographer Russell Sadur
Props stylist Rachel Jukes
Illustrator Kate Simunek
Production Controller Nigel Reed
Picture Researcher Sophie Delpech